The Walters Art Gallery
Baltimore

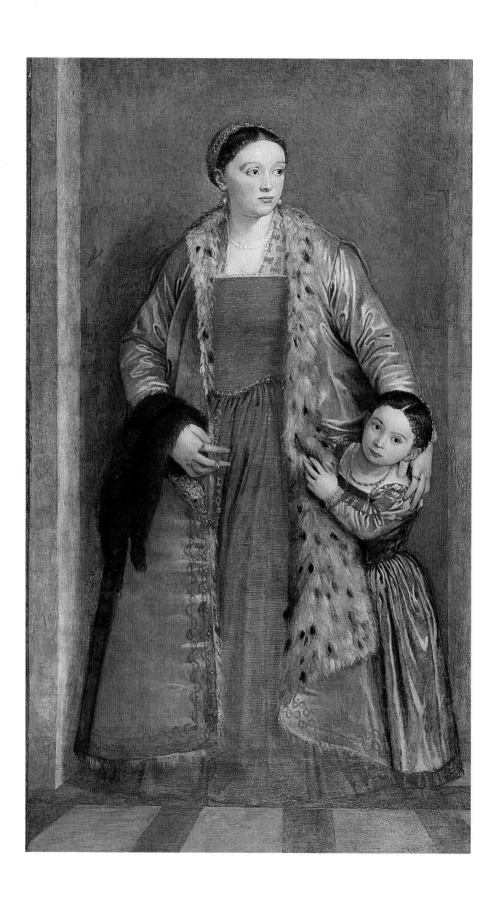

The Walters Art Gallery
Guide to the Collections

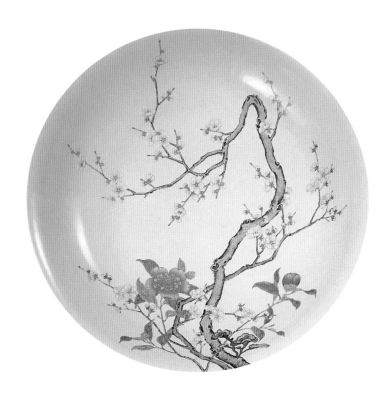

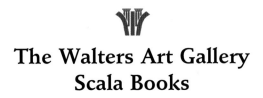

The Walters Art Gallery
Scala Books

First published in 1997 by Scala Books,
an imprint of Philip Wilson Publishers Limited
143-149 Great Portland Street London W1N 5FB

Distributed in the USA and Canada by
Antique Collectors' Club Limited
Market Street Industrial Park
Wappingers' Falls NY 12590 USA

ISBN 0-911886-48-6 (paperback edition)

Photography by Susan Tobin
Edited by Moira Johnston
Designed by Linda Wade

Printed and bound by Snoeck, Ducaju & Zoon, NV, Ghent, Belgium

List of illustrations:
Front jacket: Edouard Manet, **At the Café**, 1879
Back jacket: **Horse Head**
(Roman, first-second century AD)

Opposite title page:
Paolo Caliari, called Paolo Veronese
(Italian, Venice, 1528-88)
**Portrait of Countess Livia da Porto Thiene and
her daughter, Porzia, c. 1551**

Title page:
Dish with Flowering Prunus
(China, Ch'ing dynasty, Yung-ch'eng period, 1723-35)

Page 6:
Crozier Head with Eagle of St. John
(Italian (?), thirteenth century)
Ivory and glass paste inlay, height 8 ins (20.3 cm)
Bequest of Henry Walters, 1931; 71.300

Contents

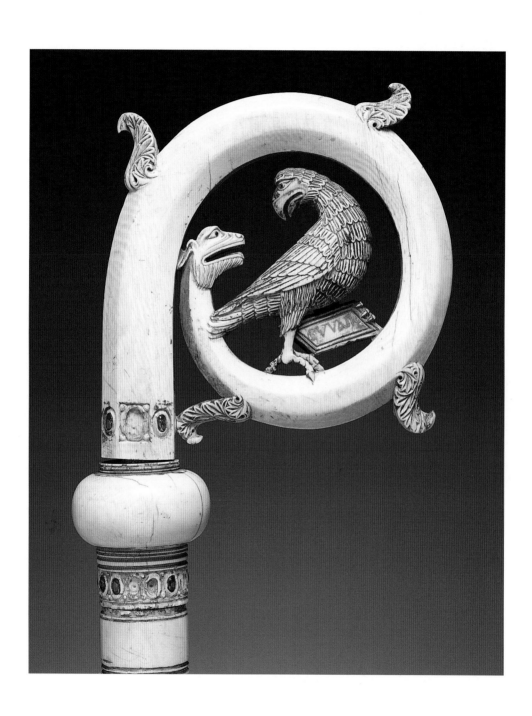

Foreword

The 170 works of art featured here represent but a minute sample of the rich holdings of the Walters Art Gallery. Long heralded as "one of the finest privately assembled museums in the United States," The Walters houses the impressive collections of western and eastern art acquired by William T. Walters of Baltimore and his son, Henry, between the 1850s and 1920s. The combined interests of father and son were culturally wide ranging, and their discerning tastes resulted in the acquisition of works of the highest aesthetic appeal and quality. When Henry Walters died in 1931, he left the City of Baltimore over 20,000 works representing virtually the full history of world civilization from 3500 BC through the early twentieth century.

At the time of Mr. Walters' magnanimous bequest, the collection was densely installed in the galleries of the palazzo-style building that he had opened to the public in 1909. Many of the works of art, however, remained in basement storage areas, including some 700 paintings and 243 crates filled with objects of every variety. Part of the transformation of Mr. Walters' treasure trove from a private collection to a public museum involved opening the crates and recording and cataloguing their contents. Even as the full measure of Mr. Walters' collection was being taken, The Walters Art Gallery was beginning to expand beyond his original generous bequest. As early as 1934 the Board of Trustees authorized its first purchases, and the expansion and enrichment of the museum's holdings have continued throughout the institution's 63-year history, thanks to acquisitions made by gift, purchase and bequest. Today the permanent collection numbers some 30,000 works of art in the fields originally collected by Henry and William Walters: ancient, medieval, Renaissance and Baroque, eighteenth and nineteenth century, Asian and Islamic art, and manuscripts and rare books.

The Walters dynamic tradition of acquisitions is fundamental to the museum's long-standing mission "to preserve, enhance, and foster understanding of the outstanding permanent collections it holds in trust for the public." Likewise, this *Guide* reflects the high standards of scholarship and art conservation research that the museum has promoted since its inception as a public institution. As with all Walters publications, its goal is—and again I quote from the mission statement—"to make the meaning and pleasures of the visual arts, their cultures and traditions, available to all."

To select 170 masterworks from collections of such breadth and depth is both a privilege and a challenge. The choice of works for this volume, and the preparation of the descriptions, involved all The Walters curators as well as research associates and museum fellows. Among the contributors, credited in the Table of Contents, William Johnston did double duty, and deserves special acknowledgement for his elegant introduction to the history of the Walters Art Gallery, based upon years of research on William and Henry Walters and their collecting passions. Likewise, Marianna Shreve Simpson both coordinated the project and wrote about our Islamic objects and manuscripts. The beautiful color reproductions are by Susan Tobin, Head of Photography, whose sensitivity to the collections is apparent on every page.

This volume results from the happy collaboration between The Walters and Philip Wilson Publishers, which has produced other titles in the museum's on-going publication program. Antony White, Managing Director, initially proposed the possibility of adding a Walters *Guide* to the prestigious Scala series. Dan Giles, Manager of Museum Publications, directed all aspects of the editorial and production process, and we are grateful to him and his staff for their efforts to present The Walters collections to fullest advantage.

It is a particular pleasure to acknowledge—with the deepest appreciation of The Walters Board of Trustees and staff—the generous support of the John J. Leidy Foundation, which came at a critical moment in the production of the *Guide* and which reflects the same commitment to the arts and dedication to the community in which Henry Walters bequeathed his incomparable collections for the benefit of the citizens of Baltimore.

Gary Vikan
Director

From Private Collection
to Public Museum

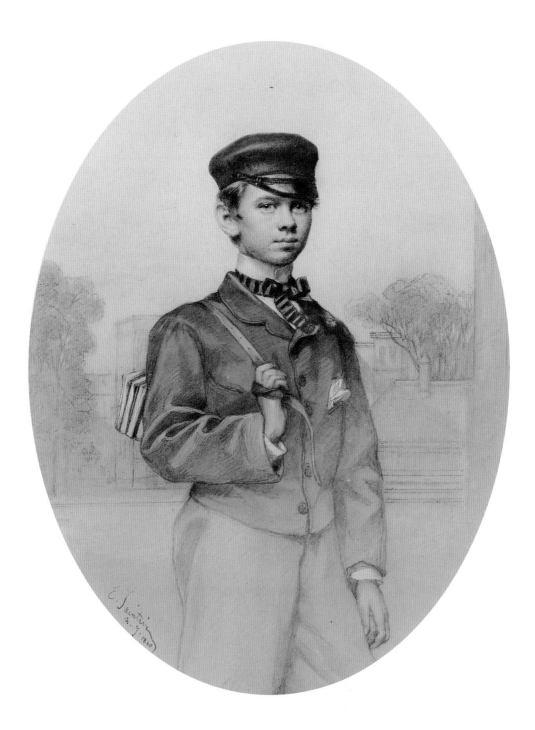

In late 1931 Baltimoreans were relieved to learn that Henry Walters (1848-1931) had bequeathed his art gallery to their city rather than to New York where he had resided much of his adult life. By the terms of his will, the Mayor and City Council received "for the benefit of the public" the gallery building, its contents, the family residence on Mount Vernon Place, and for the maintenance of these holdings, "five-twentieths" of the income of the residue of his estate. After having lagged behind other major East Coast cities in the establishment of cultural institutions, Baltimore could now claim two public art museums: the Walters Art Gallery, with its holdings of over 20,000 objects spanning four millennia, and the fledgling Baltimore Museum of Art, which had moved to its present Wyman Park address in 1929.

The Walters collection was two generations in the making. Henry's father, William Thompson Walters (1819-94), a native of the village of Liverpool in central Pennsylvania, was drawn to Baltimore in 1841. Already the hub of rail and maritime transportation systems, the city was the fastest-growing commercial center in the country. Initially Walters became a grain merchant, but by 1852 he had established a wholesale liquor house which was to become one of the largest firms of its kind

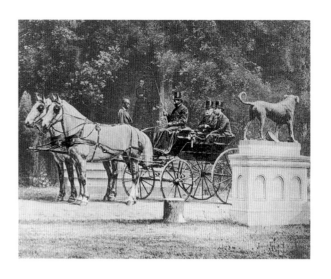

1 St. Mary's, c. 1878
William and Henry Walters in a carriage drawn by their Percheron brood mares at the Walters country estate in Govans, Maryland.

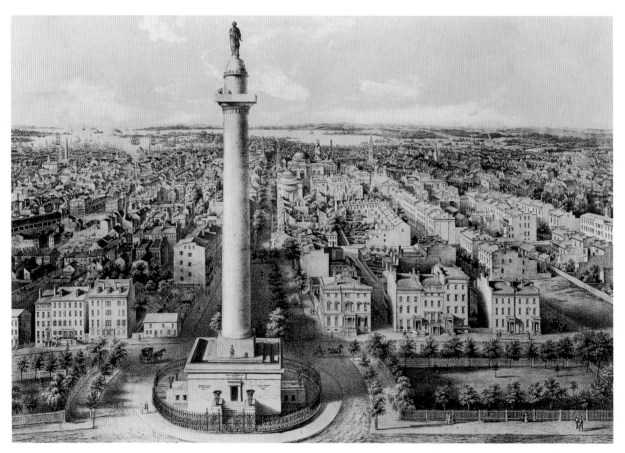

2 View of Baltimore City, 1850
Dominating the view is the Washington Monument, erected between 1815 and 1829. The first house to the right of the column was built between 1848 and 1850 for Dr. John Hanson Thomas. It is now known as Hackerman House and is used to exhibit The Walters Asian collections. Next to it, after the empty lot, is the residence that was purchased by the Walters family in 1859.

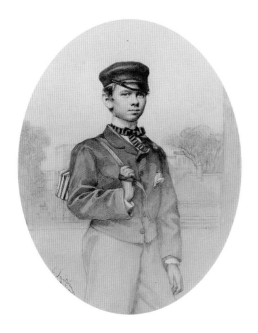

3 Jacques-Emile Saintin (French, 1829-94)
Henry Walters at age 12
Pencil and wash on cardboard
Bequest of Henry Walters, 1931.

anywhere. Six years later Walters moved to a house on Mount Vernon Place, then the most fashionable residential district in Baltimore.

At about this time Walters seriously began to collect art, initially patronizing local talents, among them Alfred Jacob Miller (1810-74) who had documented the early fur-trade in the West (page 76) and the sculptor William H. Rinehart (1825-74). Walters also sought the work of such nationally prominent artists in New York as Asher B. Durand (1796-1886), President of the National Academy of Design, and Charles Loring Elliott (1812-68), the fashionable portraitist. Unlike most other collectors of the period, he tentatively began to explore contemporary European painting, acquiring *The Duel after the Masquerade* (page 77) by Jean-Léon Gérôme, an emerging academic master in Paris.

Prior to the Civil War William Walters had outspokenly defended the right of states to secede from the Union. When the conflict erupted in 1861, he found himself in an untenable position and left the country for Europe with his wife, Ellen (1822-62) and two children, Henry and Jennie, aged thirteen and eight respectively.

Upon their arrival in Paris in the summer of 1861, they were greeted by George A. Lucas (1824-1909), a Baltimorean who four years earlier had moved to France, where he remained serving as an art consultant for a number of American clients. With Lucas as their guide, William and Ellen Walters toured the major museums and monuments and visited artists' studios, sometimes accompanied by their children. Although his income was limited, Walters patronized contemporary French artists much as he had those in Baltimore and New York,

commissioning works from Gérôme, Honoré Daumier and Antoine-Louis Barye, and from a number of *petit maîtres* whose small genre scenes and landscapes were then popular. In the autumn of 1862 the Walters family traveled to London to visit the International Exhibition. What most captivated them on this occasion were the Japanese and Chinese exhibits. The Walters family also toured the Crystal Palace, which had been moved from Hyde Park to Sydenham on the outskirts of London. Contracting a chill in the dank, cold interior, Ellen succumbed to pneumonia within several days. Her death represented a loss of a wife and mother as well as a constant companion on collecting expeditions. Although he was grief stricken, William continued to buy art, assembling two albums of drawings devoted to the subject of "prayer."

When William Walters returned to Baltimore at the close of hostilities, he enrolled his son at Georgetown College and his daughter at the Academy of the Visitation, both of which were in the District of Columbia. Subsequently Henry continued his studies at the Lawrence Scientific School in Cambridge, Massachusetts, where Jennie joined him later and attended a number of lectures at Harvard University.

Walters' business interests now shifted from liquor to banking and railroads. He was appointed a director of the Safe Deposit Company (now the Mercantile-Safe Deposit and Trust Company) and, together with several Baltimore associates, he invested in a number of railroads in the

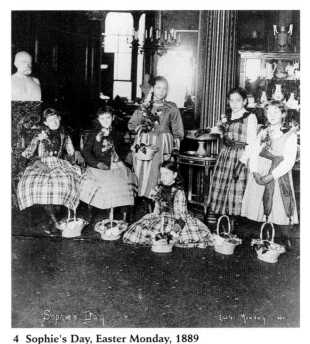

4 Sophie's Day, Easter Monday, 1889
Six young visitors were photographed in the parlor of the Walters' house during a spring opening in 1889. On the left is William H. Rinehart's portrait-bust of William Walters carved in Rome in 1867, and displayed in the vitrine on the right are some Vincennes and Sèvres porcelains.

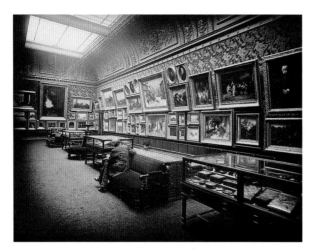

5 William T. Walters' Picture Gallery, 1884.

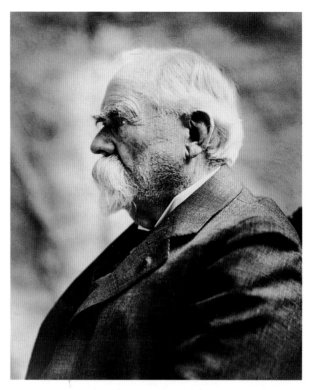

6 Photograph of Henry Walters, c. 1930.

Carolinas which eventually merged to become the Atlantic Coast Line R.R.

Meanwhile, Walters continued to expand his art collection, focusing on two fields, contemporary European painting and Asian art. Buying at auctions in New York, and relying on Lucas in Paris to transact purchases abroad (pages 73, 79), he specialized in French landscape and historical genre paintings. International exhibitions continued to attract him and he attended those held in Paris (1867 and 1878), Vienna (1873), and Philadelphia (1876). In Vienna Walters visited not only in a private capacity, but also as a commissioner representing the United States, and as chairman of the Committee on Works of Art for the Corcoran Gallery which had recently opened in Washington, DC. Many of his purchases of Asian art were undertaken at these exhibitions, particularly in 1876 and 1878. Walters' interests included Japanese lacquers, metalwork, and ceramics, especially Satsuma wares; among his Chinese acquisitions were examples of celadons and monochrome porcelains. Henry Walters, by then in his late twenties, had become his father's partner on these shopping forays, and in 1889, when William was unable to travel to Paris, he attended the exhibition in his father's place.

As early as 1874 William Walters opened the Mount Vernon Place residence to the public. Every spring, with few exceptions, he continued this civic-minded practice, charging a fee of 50 cents, with the proceeds being contributed to charity. Within a decade, when the collection had outgrown the house, he acquired an adjacent property and added a picture gallery.

The sculptures and paintings of the French master of animal subjects, Antoine-Louis Barye, remained an abiding interest. In addition to devoting a room in the house to the *animalier*'s works, in 1884 Walters donated to the city five large bronzes which were mounted in front of his house on Mount Vernon Place. These included a cast of the *Seated Lion* of the Tuileries Palace, and four replicas of sculptural groups, symbolizing *War*, *Peace*, *Order*, and *Force,* from the Louvre. Although their original locations have changed, these bronzes still stand in Mount Vernon Place, together with other sculptures given by Walters and other Baltimore art patrons.

In 1889 Henry Walters moved to Wilmington, North Carolina, to serve as general manager of his father's railroad. Following William's death in 1894, he was elected President of the Atlantic Coast Line Company and transfered the line's headquarters to New York. Henry had an uncanny flair for business and under his leadership the railroad experienced rapid growth until World War I, acquiring the vast Plant system in Florida in 1902 and taking control of the Louisville and Nashville Railroad in the same year.

In New York Henry Walters lived with Pembroke and Sarah Jones, a couple he had met in Wilmington. When time permitted he followed the Joneses on their annual perambulations to residences in Wilmington and Newport, Rhode Island. During the summers, he listed as his address the steam yacht *Narada*. Seldom did Walters return to Baltimore other than to attend board meetings of the Safe Deposit and Trust Company. Three years after Pembroke Jones' death in 1919, Henry married Sarah and they continued living in the Manhattan house surrounded by fine French eighteenth-century paintings and decorative arts and earlier Italian works of art. In his New York library Henry Walters kept many of his most prized rare books and manuscripts and other treasures.

The extraordinary scope of the collections that he assembled in Baltimore would suggest that, from the outset, Henry Walters envisaged a museum that would fulfill an educational role within the community. Initially he made modest additions to his father's collection. Benefiting from historical perspective, he enhanced the

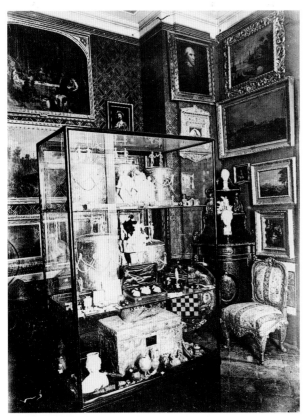

7 The Palazzo Accoramboni, before 1902
Don Marcello Massarenti stored his collection in the Palazzo
Accoramboni, Rome. The Palazzo was razed in the 1930s to
make way for the Via della Conciliazione. Displayed in the
central vitrine is a Praenestine *cista* (page 29).

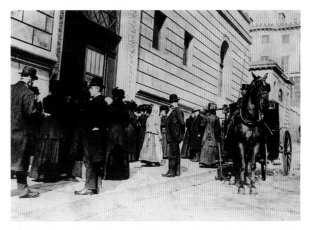

8 The Opening of Henry Walters' Gallery, 3 February 1909

he bought the contents of the Palazzo Accoramboni in
Rome. These had been assembled over fifty years by Don
Marcello Massarenti (1817-1905), a priest who served as
under-almoner, or fiduciary secretary, to the Holy See. In
anticipation of selling his collection, Massarenti had
published a two-part catalogue listing 865 paintings,
principally by early Italian and northern artists, as well as
a number of antiquities, mostly of Roman origin. Many of
the attributions were overly ambitious, which imparted a
somewhat unsavory reputation to the collection. Despite
the mis-identifications, the collection abounded in works
of significance. Many of them were by masters other than
those to whom they had been ascribed, and others were
by artists not at that time in fashion. In the latter category
fell El Greco's painting *St. Francis receiving the Stigmata*
(page 54). Among Massarenti's archeological treasures
were seven magnificent sarcophagi from a burial chamber
associated with the Calpurnii Pisones family, pieces that
alone would have justified the purchase of the collection

breadth of the nineteenth-century holdings with such
early works as Ingres' *Betrothal of Raphael* (page 69),
bought in 1903. Although he did not find French
Impressionism to his liking, he agreed in that year to buy
two examples from Mary Cassat—Monet's *Springtime*, an
exquisite image of the artist's wife, Camille, seated on the
grass beneath lilac bushes in their garden at Argenteuil
(page 80), and a small Degas portrait. Likewise, he
continued his father's practice of attending the
international exhibitions, where he gravitated to the
works of contemporary, prize-winning artists. At the
Louisiana Purchase Exposition in St. Louis in 1904, he
bought some works from the Japanese Pavilion, the most
expensive of which was a tapestry of a thirteenth-century
battle from the workshop of Kawasaki Jimbei II, the
recipient of a grand prize that year (page 98).

That Henry's ambitions for the collection far
exceeded his father's became apparent in 1900 when he
bought Raphael's *Madonna of the Candelabra* (page 51), a
tondo which had passed through both the Borghese and
Bonaparte family collections. Also that year he purchased
a number of properties on Charles Street, in Mount
Vernon Place, to serve as a site for a future gallery.

Two years later Henry undertook an acquisition on a
scale unprecedented in the history of American collecting:

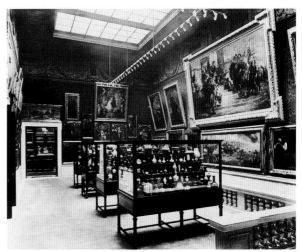

9 The West Gallery, Henry Walters' Gallery, 1909
Mounted on the west wall are Maerten van Heemskerck's
Panoramic Fantasy with the Abduction of Helen (page 60), and
above, Giovanni Battista Tiepolo's *Scipio Africanus freeing Massiva*
(page 57). Chinese ceramics and Japanese lacquers were
displayed in cases throughout the galleries.

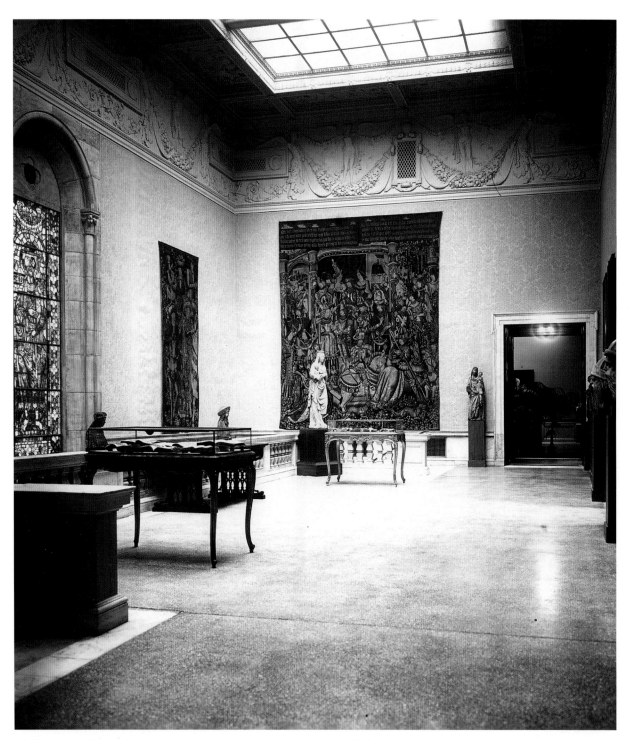

10 The Foyer (formerly the West Gallery),
The Walters Art Gallery, 1935

Sarah Walters' son-in-law, John Russell Pope, designed the
Romanesque-style frames for the stained-glass windows.

(page 31). Undeterred by the rumors he had heard, Henry
hastened to Rome with his friend and advisor William
Laffan (1848-1909), and after they had viewed the works
under extremely unfavorable conditions—they were
densely installed from floor to ceiling and inadequately
lighted—he courageously agreed to buy the collection for
the sum of five million FF or $1,000,000. A steamship, the

SS Minterne, was then chartered to transport the art works
to New York.

Now possessing the core of a museum collection,
Walters had to construct a suitable building to house it. He
chose as his architect William Adams Delano (1874-1960),
a young family friend who had only just received a
diploma from the Ecole des Beaux-Arts in Paris. Delano

proposed a palazzo-like structure inspired in its interior by the early seventeenth-century Collegio dei Gesuiti (now the Palazzo dell'Università) in Genoa. For the exterior he looked to Paris, specifically to Félix Duban's nineteenth-century Hôtel Pourtalès. Ground was broken on Charles Street in 1905, and two and a half years later the building was ready to receive the collection.

When the first public reception was held in the new gallery in 1909, the installations of the collections already appeared crowded. Undeterred, Henry Walters continued to augment his holdings, buying both in New York and abroad. From time to time he expressed an intent to winnow his holdings, and in 1909 he first consulted with Bernard Berenson (1865-1959). The eminent authority categorized the Massarenti pictures as "good, bad, and indifferent," and suggested that some should be withdrawn. Walters, however, could not bear to part with any, although the most egregious copies were assigned to storage. Berenson also recommended that he obtain a number of additions, including a remarkably intact altarpiece showing the *Annunciation* painted by the early fifteenth-century heir to the Giottesque traditions, Bicci di Lorenzo (page 50).

Every year in late spring Henry Walters set off for his European shopping forays, first visiting specific dealers in Paris. Usually he started with Dikran Kelekian (1868-1951) whom he had met at the World's Columbian Exposition in Chicago in 1893. The Armenian dealer subsequently opened shops in Paris and New York and would become a principal source for Egyptian, ancient Near Eastern, and Islamic art, as well as for a number of key classical and western medieval objects. Among the latter, the most spectacular was a pair of limestone heads of Old Testament rulers that had come from the the abbey church of Saint-Denis, just north of Paris (page 41). In 1897 the purchase of a fifteenth-century Koran, originally thought to be Persian, but now regarded as Indian (page 122), may have initiated the manuscript collection. On the same trip, Walters bought a seventeenth-century Turkish tile showing a bird's-eye view of the Great Mosque in Mecca (page 108). Kelekian continued to provide Walters with antiquities, among the most memorable of which were an Egyptian gilded mummy mask dating from the Roman period (page 22) and a marble head of Augustus also said to have been found in Egypt (page 31), both bought in 1913.

Henry Walters often frequented the establishment of Jacques Seligmann (1858-1923) on the Place Vendôme, Paris, which dealt in Gothic carved ivories (page 45), Italian majolica, sixteenth-century Limoges enamels, and eighteenth-century decorative arts. As a result of a family feud, the Seligmann firm was divided, but Henry Walters

11 The Walters Art Gallery, 1974
The extension was designed by Shepley, Bulfinch, Richardson and Abbott of Boston and Meyer, Ayres and Saint of Baltimore.

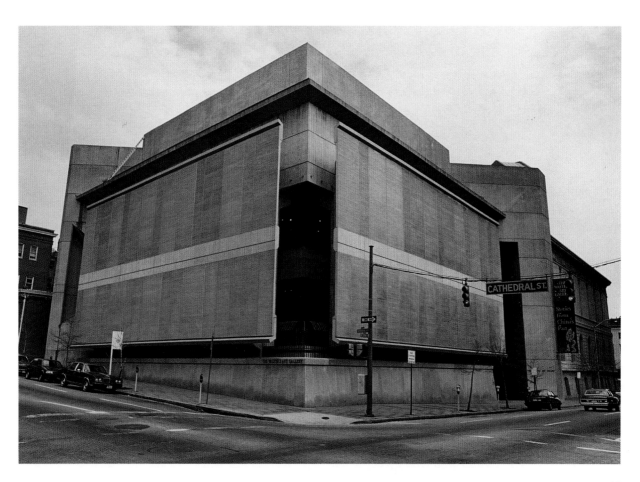

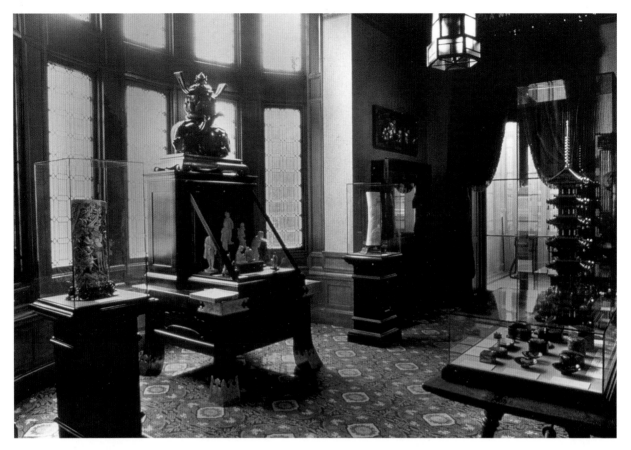

12 The Interior of Hackerman House, 1991
The house, once the property of William T. Walters' neighbour, Dr. John Hanson Thomas, is now used for the display of the Gallery's Asian holdings.

continued to patronize both offshoots, acquiring a significant portion of his collection through them.

Another invariable stop on Henry Walters' annual Paris pilgrimage was the shop of Léon Gruel (1841-1923). Originally a dealer in marriage and communion albums, Gruel became known for book-bindings, medieval manuscripts, and rare books. In addition to providing Walters with many manuscripts, Gruel was responsible for a number of the medieval carved ivories that entered the collection.

Henry Walters sometimes continued from Paris to Venice to visit another dealer in early printed books and manuscripts, Leo S. Olschki (1861-1940). In 1903 he purchased an entire "wallful" of over a thousand incunabula (books printed before 1501) with the stipulation that Olschki finish cataloguing them. *Incunabula Typographica* was printed in 1905, the year that Olschki sold Walters an exceptional thirteenth-century Bible (page 112) commissioned in Sicily for the boy-emperor Conradin whose execution in 1268 ended the Hohenstaufen line in Italy.

In New York, beginning in 1903, Henry Walters served on the executive committee of the Metropolitan Museum of Art and ten years later he became second Vice-President, a position he retained for the rest of his life. His experiences on a number of museum committees may have resulted in a change of direction in his collecting

after World War I. Walters now appeared less concerned with acquiring works representative of various fields and more committed to objects of major historical and artistic significance. One of his most outstanding purchases was a panel showing a contemplative *Donor with St. John the Baptist* painted in minute detail by the Flemish artist Hugo van der Goes (page 62). It was acquired from Jacques Seligmann in 1920. That year Walters also enriched his Asian holdings with several early, large-scale sculptures purchased through Yamanaka & Company, a firm of antiquarians from Osaka, Japan, with shops in New York and Boston. At the New York branch he bought a painted and lacquered wooden image of the seated Buddha from the Sui dynasty (page 89) which is said to have come from a Buddhist temple in Cheng-ting, Hopei.

After World War I, Joseph Brummer (1883-1947) and his brothers, Ernest and Imre, opened galleries in New York and Paris. Their varied stock provided Walters with an alternative to that of Kelekian for many fields. It was from Brummer, for example, that he bought a hammered and carved silver bowl showing an enthroned king, attendants, and dancing girls (page 100), which is now thought to have been made in Iran during the early Islamic era (seventh century or later). One of Walters' last major purchases from Brummer was a collection of twenty-three pieces of early Christian silver including a chalice (page 35) which was first photographed in 1910 in Hama, Syria, but which has since then been identified as having come from the church of St. Sergios in Kaper Koraon in northern Syria.

Following Henry Walters' death in 1931, the Mayor of Baltimore appointed a board of trustees who, in turn, consulted with a distinguished committee of museum personnel and scholars regarding the proper management of a public museum. Within a year a research staff of five curators, a conservator, and a chemist had been appointed. The Gallery very briefly re-opened in the spring of 1934 to allow visitors to view for the last time the outdated, cluttered installations of the Henry Walters' era. It was then closed to provide the staff with an opportunity to transform the Gallery completely into a modern, public institution.

Over the summer the curators catalogued the collections, prepared a handbook, and began to organize a number of pioneering exhibitions. Inevitably their efforts were constrained by the lack of adequate space to display the collections. Nevertheless the Gallery continued to

augment its holdings through purchases and gifts, albeit at a modest pace. Among the rareties that Henry Walters had kept in his New York library was an early thirteenth-century Gospel book (page 120) by Tòros Roslin, the most gifted artist from the Armenian kingdom of Cilicia. Sarah Walters donated the manuscript to the Gallery in 1935. Four years later she sold to Baltimore, for the price her husband had originally paid, a double panel of a Netherlandish altar from the Carthusian monastery of Champmol near Dijon, France (page 58). When Sarah Walters auctioned many of the works from her New York residence in 1941, the Walters trustees voted to bid for eleven of them, including a large, late antique vase carved out of a single agate (page 34) which had been taken as plunder from Constantinople by French crusaders in 1204. Subsequently it had passed through a number of distinguished collections, most notably that of the artist and diplomat Peter-Paul Rubens (1517-1640).

The first large donation to the Gallery came in 1963 when a collection of over four hundred European and

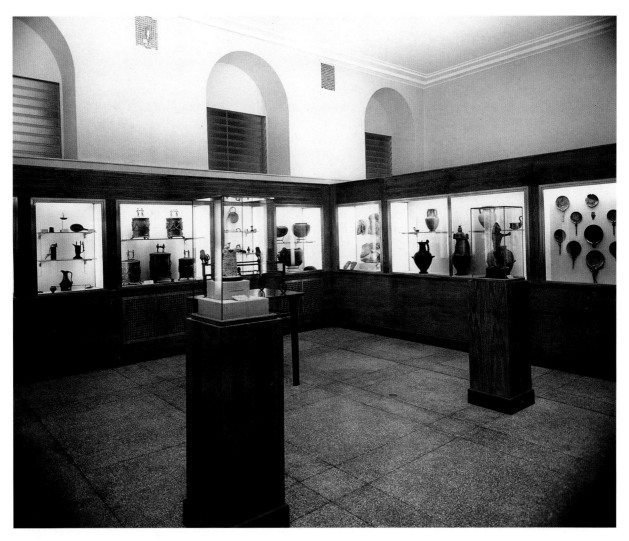

13 The Etruscan, Late Classical and Barbarian Gallery, c. 1935

Visible in one of the wall cases on the left is the Praenestine *cista* which appeared in the photograph of the interior of the Accoramboni Palace.

American portrait miniatures assembled by a local business leader, Abraham Jay Fink (1890-1963), was presented to the Gallery. Most of the miniatures dated from the eighteenth and nineteenth centuries, although there were also a number of earlier examples including a pair of portraits painted by the Utrecht artist Cornelis van Poelenburch to commemorate the 1626 marriage of Jan Pellicorne and Susanna van Collen (page 63).

The Gallery's initial purchase policy was to enhance those aspects of the collection that were inadequately represented rather than to emphasize existing strengths. To augment its Flemish holdings, for example, the Gallery purchased in 1948 a seventeenth-century view of the Infanta Isabella of Spain and her husband, the Archduke Albert, visiting a collector's cabinet of natural curiosities and artistic treasures (page 63). The authorship of this work, which once belonged to Walters' rival collector and business associate, J. Pierpont Morgan (1837-1913), has been debated, but is now identified as Frans Francken II and workshop, with Jan Brueghel II.

In 1972 the Gallery fortuitously reunited a pair of Canaanite bronze figurines from the early second millennium BC (page 23) which had been separated in 1919. Likewise, ten years later, the Gallery acquired a sixteenth-century Venetian gold marten's head (page 53), nearly identical to one appearing mounted on a pelt in Paolo Veronese's *Portrait of Countess Livia da Porto Thiene and her Daughter, Porzia* (page 53).

Attempts to win financial support for a major building expansion failed in 1958 and the 1960s. Only in 1966 did Baltimore City's passage of a bond issue, together with a grant from the State of Maryland and private contributions, enable the Gallery to realize plans for more exhibition space. Shepley, Bulfinch, Richardson and Abbott of Boston, and Meyer, Ayres and Saint of Baltimore were chosen to design a new wing. Their plans called for an exterior with expansive surfaces of raw concrete which would complement the masonry walls of the Delano building, and for an interior with a series of intimate galleries in which to view the many small objects in the collection.

The opening of the extension in 1974 not only resulted in greater display space and permitted an expansion of programs, but also stimulated the growth of the collections. The previous year Dr. Francis D. Murnaghan of Baltimore arranged for a gift of eighteen Renaissance and Baroque paintings from the collection of his brother, the Dublin collector, Judge James A. Murnaghan (1882-1973). Among them was the magnificent painting, *The Parable of the Wheat and the Tares* by Abraham Bloemaert (page 62). Another member of the same family, the Honorable Francis D. Murnaghan, Jr., presented four Irish paintings including Jack B. Yeats' *The Swinford Funeral, 1918* (page 84), which gives a *terminus ante quem* for the Gallery's painting collection.

An acquisitions fund established by the W. Alton Jones Foundation in 1983 enabled the Gallery to purchase a number of major works in a variety of fields. These included an Indian bronze statue of Krishna from the late tenth century (page 86), a Hellenistic marble head (page 27), Guido Reni's masterpiece, *The Penitent Magdalene* (page 55), and a long and complex handscroll, *Free Spirits among the Streams and Mountains*, by Wang Yüan-ch'i (page 91).

More recently Mr. and Mrs. Willard Hackerman presented to the City of Baltimore a house on Mount Vernon Place adjacent to the original Gallery. When built between 1848 and 1850 for Dr. John Hanson Thomas, this residence was described as "one of the most elegant and princely specimens of architectural taste and mechanical skill." Still ranked among the most handsome, late-classical structures in the city, the house was entrusted by the City to The Walters Art Gallery to be used to exhibit Asian art. Local collectors of Asian art have responded by donating a number of significant works. Among them are a fourteenth- to fifteenth-century bronze statue of the Hindu god Shiva (page 86), given by John and Berthe Ford in 1988, and a twelfth-century sandstone figure of a female deity from Cambodia (page 88), presented by Lispenard and Marshall Green in 1994.

The most remarkable addition to the Asian holdings has been the Alexander B. Griswold collection of the Breezewood Foundation, Monkton, which was transfered to The Walters Art Gallery in 1992. Griswold first visited Thailand at the close of World War II and subsequently maintained a residence in Bangkok. Not only did he become a noted authority on Thai art, but he also assembled a fully representative collection of Thai sculptures and paintings. In addition he selected related works from the cultures of Cambodia, India, and other Southeast Asian countries. Although Griswold had already donated works, his 1992 bequest resulted in The Walters collection of Thai sculpture becoming the most extensive in the United States. The breadth of his interests is demonstrated by a sandstone standing Buddha from Thailand in the eighth century (page 87), a fifteenth-century Buddha in leaded bronze from North-central Thailand (page 87), a Gandharan statue of a seated Buddha (page 86), and a late twelfth- to early thirteenth-century Cambodian represention of an eight-armed Bodhisattva, Avalokiteshvara (page 88). The Walters Asian holdings and their recent growth have been more fully documented in a separate publication (Hiram W. Woodward, Jr., *Asian Art in The Walters Art Gallery, A Selection*, Baltimore, 1991).

Adhering to Henry Walters' commitment to comprehensiveness, the Gallery continues to expand its holdings, exploring fields not readily available earlier in the century. Most recently, seventeen examples of Ethiopian art ranging in date from the fourteenth to the nineteenth centuries have been acquired. Among the highlights is a large, late fifteenth-century liturgical fan showing the figure of Mary, archangels and apostles (page 39) which was purchased in 1996 with the W. Alton Jones Foundation Acquisition Fund.

The Walters Art Gallery continues to examine its changing role within the community and seeks to determine how it may best serve the public's interests. Meanwhile, the collections will undoubtedly flourish, expanding both in scope and depth.

Ancient Art

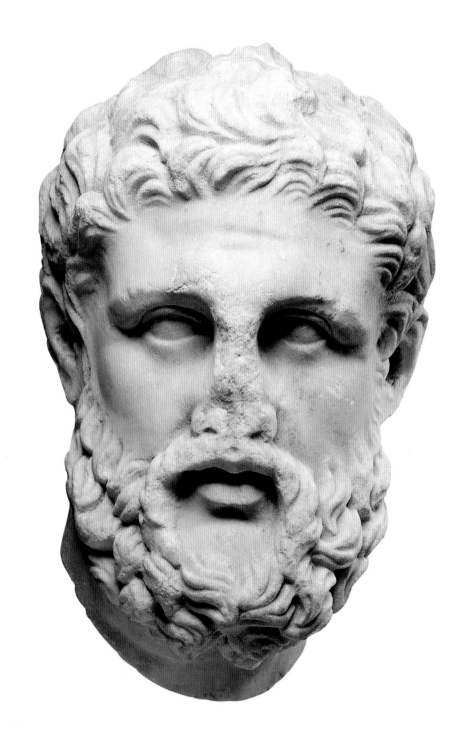

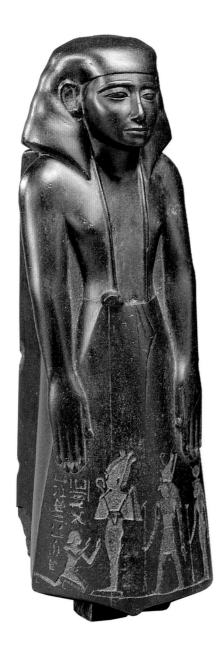

Statues of Nenkhefetkai and Neferseshemes
(Egyptian, Old Kingdom, Fifth Dynasty, c. 2465-2323 BC)
Limestone, height without base 19 ½ ins (49.5 cm)
Acquired by exchange with the Museum of Fine Arts,
Boston, 1973; 22.425

Found in a rock-cut tomb at Deshasheh, located about
seventy miles to the south of modern Cairo, this pair-
statue of the mayor Nenkhefetkai and his wife
Neferseshemes exemplifies in the pose and relative scale
of its subjects the standard Egyptian artistic conventions
for the representation of men and women. Nenkhefetkai
strides forward with his left foot and holds his arms
closely at his sides, while his wife is depicted on a
smaller scale and stands with her feet together. Each
statue was carved separately and altered prior to burial
to fit into a shared base.

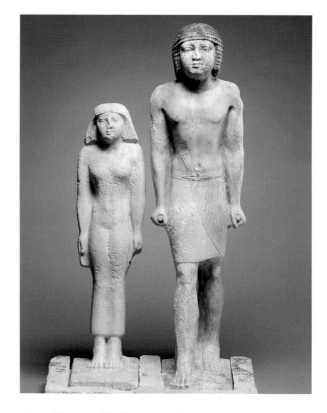

Seated Statue of Enehey (opposite)
(Egyptian, New Kingdom, c. 1333-1290 BC)
Limestone, height 51 ¹⁵⁄₁₆ ins (132 cm)
Bequest of Henry Walters, 1931; 22.106

Depicted much as she would have appeared in life,
the Chantress Enehey sits on a chair and holds in her
left hand the symbol of her profession, a *sistrum* or rattle
used in the worship of the goddess Hathor. Judging
from her fine clothing and elegant hairstyle, as well
as the scale and quality of her statue, we may assume
that Enehey was able to afford a fine burial to ensure
her place in the afterlife. Most likely this statue, one of
only two known, graced a tomb at Memphis, the ancient
capital of Egypt.

Statue of a High Official, reinscribed for Pa-di-iset
(Egyptian, Middle Kingdom, Twelfth Dynasty, c. 1991-1783 BC)
(inscription c. 945-712 BC)
Basalt, height 12 ins (30.5 cm)
Bequest of Henry Walters, 1931; 22.203

A remarkable example of the re-use of a work of art,
reflecting the course of Egypt's long history, this statue
was originally carved to commemorate a powerful
government official. More than a thousand years later
the inscription naming this unknown man was erased,
and a carved scene was added depicting its new owner,
Pa-di-iset, son of Apy, worshipping the gods Osiris,
Horus, and Isis. From a text on the rear of the statue we
learn that Pa-di-iset was a diplomatic messenger to the
neighboring lands of Canaan and Peleset (Palestine).

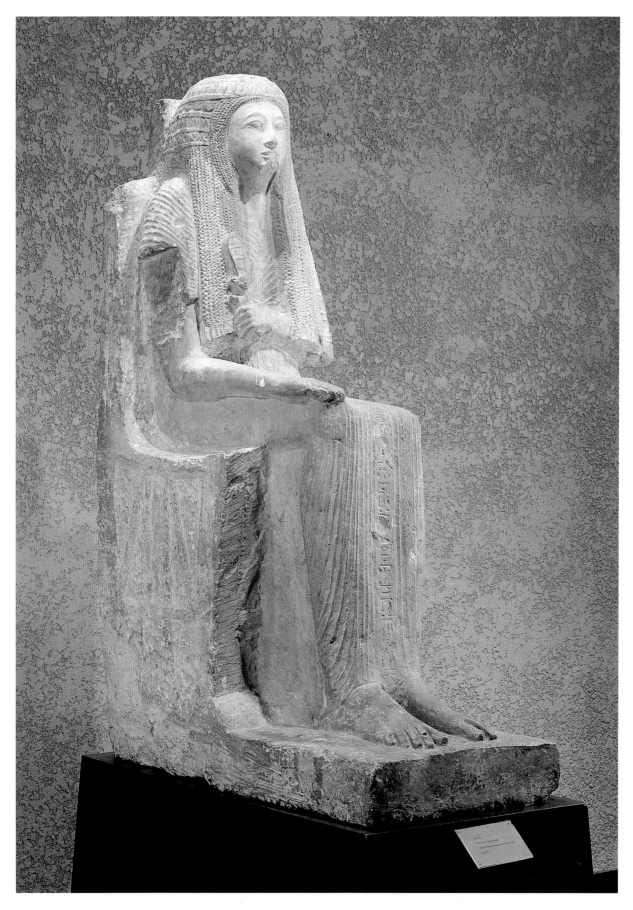

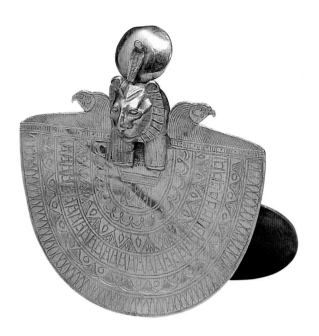

Cultic Ornament of a Lion-Headed Goddess
(Egyptian, Third Intermediate Period, c. 700 BC)
Gold, height 2 ¾ ins (7 cm)
Bequest of Henry Walters, 1931; 57.540

The collars worn by both Egyptian men and women were composed of two main parts: in front, a broad collar made from floral elements, and a counterpoise falling behind the neck to balance the weight of the collar. The head of a feline goddess atop this model collar indicates that it is intended as a personification of her powers, conveying in its decoration the ability of the lioness (here probably Wadjet) both to protect and to nourish the king who might have been its owner. Her dual nature is evoked by her stern and watchful face on the front side, and by her representation as a mother suckling a young prince on the reverse.

Gilded Mummy Mask with Glass Inlays
(Egyptian, Roman Period, late first century BC)
Cartonnage, gold leaf and glass, height 20 ½ ins (52 cm)
Bequest of Henry Walters, 1931; 78.3

Although Roman art had already exerted a strong influence on the traditional art of Egypt by the first century of the common era, this mask which once covered the linen wrappings of a mummy, demonstrates the survival of powerful religious and artistic concepts. The gilded face reflects the assimilation of the deceased with the sun god, while inlays in glass depicting a sacred ibis and scarab beetle relate to Pharaonic ideas of spiritual rebirth and renewal.

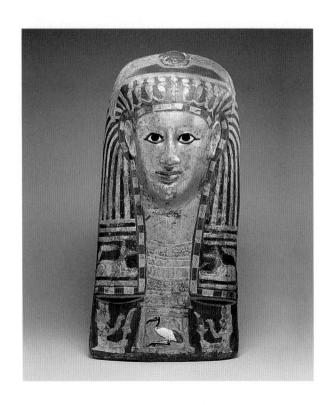

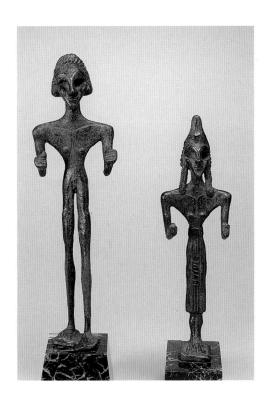

Figurines of Baal and Anat
(Canaanite, early second millennium BC)
Bronze, height 9 ⅟₁₆ ins (23 cm) and 7 ¾ ins (19.8 cm)
Bequest of Henry Walters, 1931; 54.788; Museum Purchase, 1972; 54.2487

These solid cast figurines served as votive offerings. The male figure represents the Canaanite war god, Baal, bringer of the autumnal rains and suppressor of the destructive flood waters. He probably wore a gold skirt and may have carried a mace in one of his clenched fists. The female is surely Anat, a fertility goddess who is the sister and consort of Baal.

Relief with Winged Genius
(Assyrian, 883-859 BC)
Alabaster, height 93 ⁹⁄₁₆ ins (237.6 cm)
Bequest of Henry Walters, 1931; 21.8

This relief decorated the interior wall of the palace of King Ashurnasirpal at Nimrud, which is now situated in present-day Iraq. With his right hand the genius, or benevolent spirit, uses a cone-shaped object to sprinkle from his bucket some magic potion upon either a sacred tree or the king depicted on the adjacent relief. The genius wears the horned crown of a divinity and the elegant jewelry and fringed cloak of contemporary courtiers.

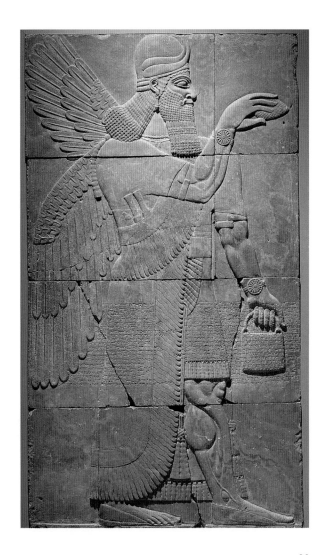

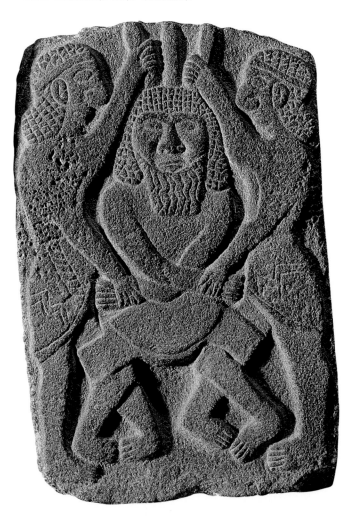

Relief from Tel Halaf
(North Syria, c. ninth century BC)
Basalt, height 24 ⁷⁄₁₆ ins (62.2 cm)
Museum Purchase, 1944; 21.18

This relief decorated the lower course of
the exterior wall of the temple palace of King
Kapara. Two heroes pin down a bearded foe,
while grabbing at his pronged headdress. The
composition was probably borrowed from the
decorative arts and is rendered here as a flat
raised surface with incised linear details.

Stand in the Shape of a Wild Goat
(Iran (Azerbaijan), c. eighth century BC)
Bronze, height 12 ins (30.5 cm)
Museum Purchase, 1949; 54.2328

The ring above the horns supported a bowl that may
have held offerings or incense. No exact parallel is
known for this unusual piece, and the ultimate
inspiration may lie in the central Asian steppes.

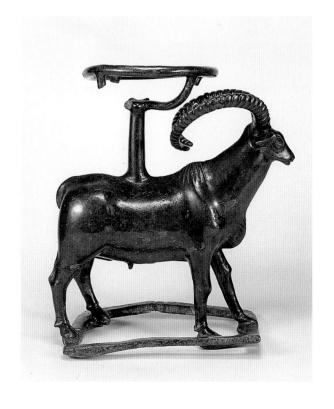

Figurine of a Maiden
(Greek, c. 675-650 BC)
Bronze, height 7 ⅛ ins (18 cm)
Bequest of Henry Walters, 1931; 54.773

This maiden's horizontal layers of hair, simple facial features, and unarticulated form indicate that she was fashioned before the advent of large-scale marble sculpture. She may have been a votive offering, possibly to the goddess Artemis. The cutting away behind her legs may indicate that she formed part of an attachment, perhaps grouped with two companions as a stand to support a vase.

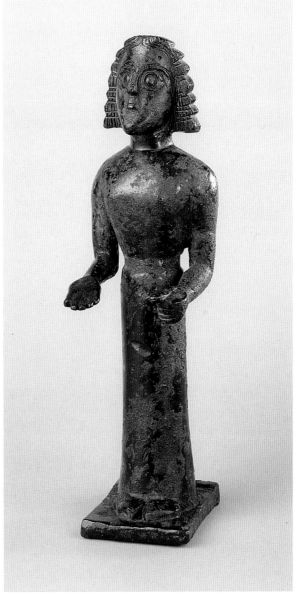

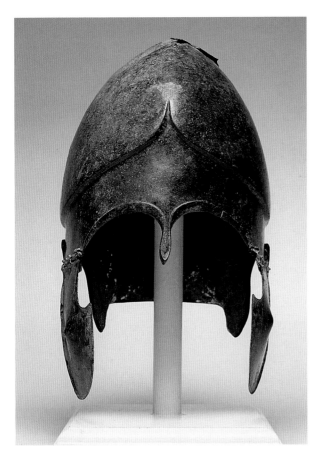

Helmet
(Greek, c. 500 BC)
Bronze, height 12 ins (30.5 cm)
Museum Purchase, 1966; 54.2468

The form of this helmet, known as Chalcidian, is distinguished by the curved cheekpieces which are attached here by pins terminating in snake heads. The advance in Greek technology that made possible the widespread production of hammered bronze helmets also led to the mass production of shields. As a result, on the battlefield individual duels were superseded by the phalanx, a form of combat in which warriors advanced together as an almost impenetrable wall of weaponry.

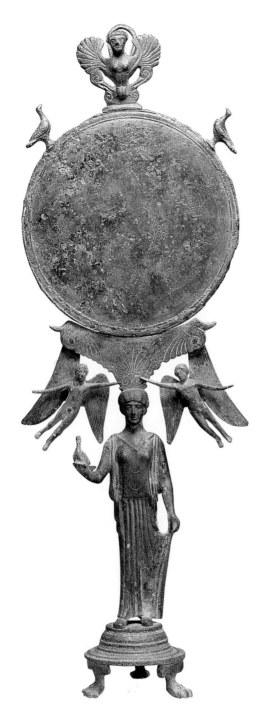

Caryatid Mirror
(Greek, c. 460 BC)
Bronze, height 16 ⅞ ins (43 cm)
Bequest of Henry Walters, 1931; 54.769

The mirror disc would have been silvered to provide
a reflective surface. The calm pose, gesture, and
drapery epitomize the quiet elegance of the
classical style. The presence of the flying Erotes
suggests that the maiden is Aphrodite. The Siren
at the top of the disc reminded the owner of the
magnetic allure of the mythical bird-women,
whose songs enticed men to their deaths.

Attic Red-figure Amphora by the Niobid Painter
(Attic, Greek, c. 460-450 BC)
Clay, height 17 ¹³⁄₁₆ ins (45.3 cm)
Museum Purchase, 1993; 48.2712

One of the prominent painters of classical Athens, this
artist is admired for his elegant compositions and
harmonious balance of light and dark. In the women's
quarters of a house a woman relaxes upon a klismos
while fingering a barbiton (a stringed instrument). Above
her head hangs a lyre. The woman in front of her holds
the double flutes, and the woman behind lifts the lid of a
box, which probably contained book rolls.

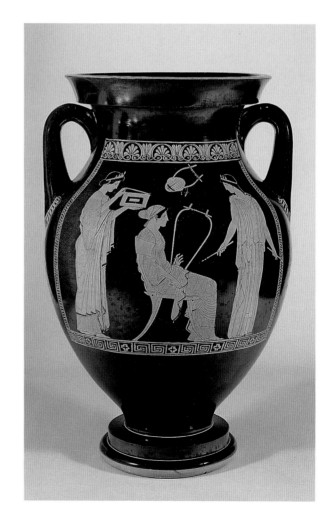

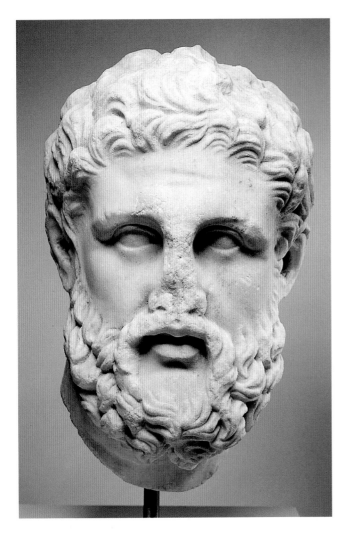

Head of a Man from a Funerary Relief
(Greek, c. 325-317 BC)
Marble, height 12 ¹¹⁄₁₆ ins (32.3 cm)
Museum Purchase through W. Alton Jones
Foundation Acquisition Fund, 1986; 23.239

This head belonged to a type of Attic grave
monument in which images of family members
were presented as a tableau within a stage-like
niche. The deep-set eyes, furrowed brow, and
tousled hair are characteristic of the art of the
Hellenistic period, the beginning of which is dated
to the death of Alexander the Great in 323 BC.

Bracelet from Olbia
(Hellenistic, Greek,
late second century BC)
Gold, garnet, amethyst, chrysoprase,
pearl white and blue glass, and red,
blue, green and turquoise enamel,
height 2 ¹⁄₁₆ ins (5.2cm)
Bequest of Henry Walters, 1931;
57.375

This bracelet reflects the
elaborate ornaments worn
in the courts of Hellenistic
rulers. The emphasis on
polychromy was an indirect
result of the conquests of
Alexander the Great (died 323
BC), which released Persian
treasures of precious gems and
introduced the Greek world to
the traditional oriental taste for
colored gemstones.

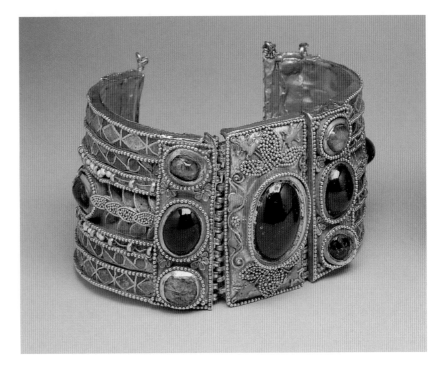

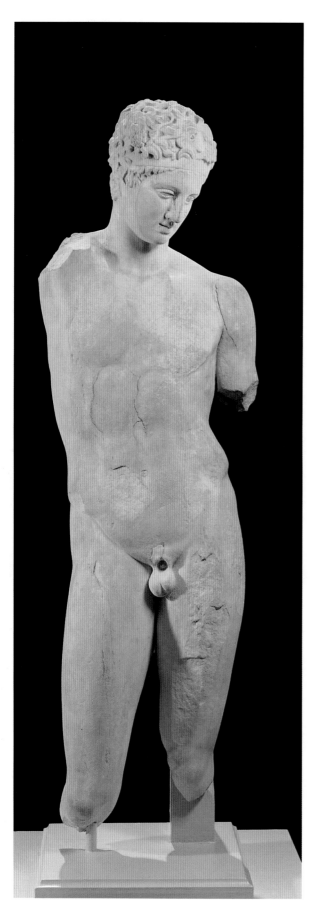

Pouring Satyr
(Roman copy after a bronze original of 370-360 BC)
Marble, height 44 ins (106.7 cm)
Bequest of Henry Walters, 1931; 23.22

The original bronze statue, now lost, was by the celebrated artist Praxiteles, whose satyr, a follower of the wine-god Dionysos, poured from a jug in his upraised right hand into a phiale in his extended left hand. The sinuous curves and unmuscled adolescent body are closely associated with Praxiteles, as is the light-hearted tone of the subject.

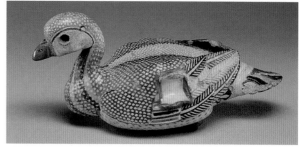

Vase in the Shape of a Duck
(Hellenistic, Alexandrian, third-second century BC)
Faience, length 7 ins (17.5 cm)
Bequest of Henry Walters, 1931; 48.421

There are remains of a ring handle on the bird's side. Faience is a product of ground quartz and natron (sodium carbonate and sodium bicarbonate). The addition of copper oxide precipitates a self-glazing process, which takes place during firing. Most faience is a blue or green color, and thus the blue-gray, yellow, brown, and white seen here are unusual. The form may have been inspired by the red-figure duck vases of Etruria and south Italy.

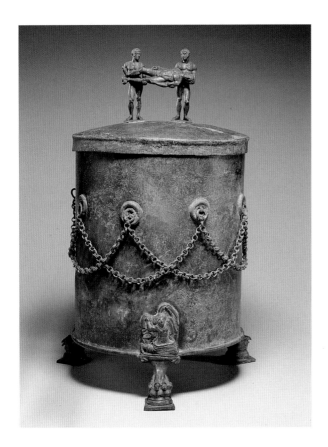

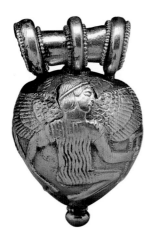

Cista
(Praenestine, fourth century BC)
Bronze, height 14 ¾ ins (37.5 cm)
Bequest of Henry Walters, 1931; 54.136

Cistae were used to safeguard precious objects, including a woman's toiletries. The elaborate engraved scenes are usually thought to reflect famous, and now lost, Greek wallpaintings. Seen here is the story of the mythical Perseus, who holds the head of the gorgon Medusa. On the handle a reclining man is supported by two other men; this incorporation of the human figure into a functional object indicates influence from the neighboring Etruscan civilization.

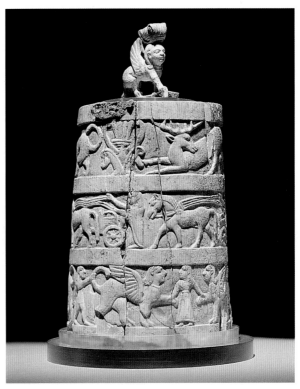

Pyxis with Sphinx Finial
(Etruscan, 650-625 BC)
Ivory, height 5 ½ ins (14 cm)
Bequest of Henry Walters, 1931; 71.489

This pyxis (cylindrical container) was probably made in Etruria after Near Eastern models. Eastern motifs include sphinxes, a lotus plant, and a Phoenician palmette. The pyxis was found in Cerveteri (northwest of Rome) near the famous Regolini-Galassi tomb, where a very similar example was recovered.

Bulla with Dedalus
(Etruscan, fifth century BC)
Gold, height 1 %6 ins (4 cm)
Bequest of Henry Walters, 1931; 57.371

The bulla was a decorative and protective pendant; found inside this example was labdanum, a substance used to fix scents. Depicted in *repoussé* is the mythical craftsman Dedalus, who carries the saw and adze that he was said to have invented. On the opposite side is his son, Icarus, for whom the father fashioned marvellous wings. When Icarus disobeyed his father's instructions and flew too close to the sun, the heat melted the wax attaching the wings to his body, and the boy plunged downward to his death.

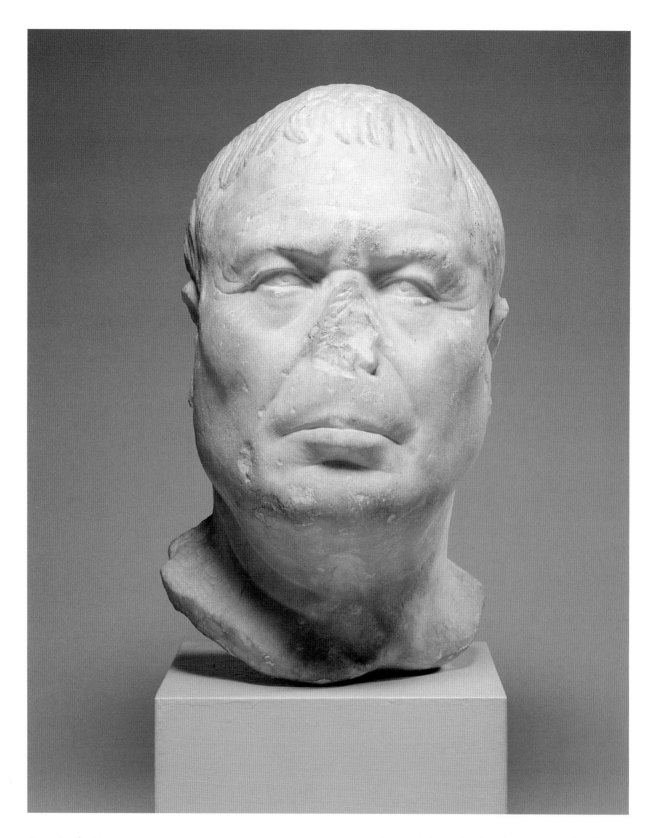

Portrait of a Man
(Roman, Republican, c. 40 BC)
Marble, height 12 ins (30.5 cm)
Bequest of Henry Walters,
1931; 23.209

A carved portrait from the decades just preceding the consolidation of the Republic into the Empire, this head, through its lined face and tight-lipped gaze, evokes determination, experience, and pragmatism, qualities thought to epitomize the Romans' national character.

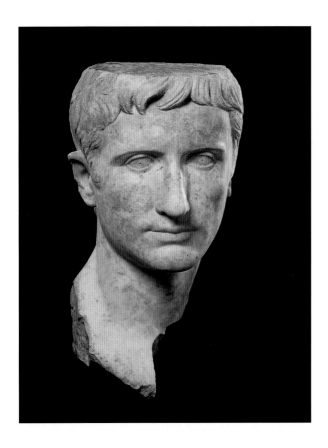

Head of Augustus
(Roman, 27 BC-14 AD)
Marble, height 15 ⅞ ins (41.2 cm)
Bequest of Henry Walters, 1931; 23.21

After the youthful Augustus (63 BC-14 AD) consolidated
Roman power and established what became known as
the Empire, he attempted to re-create classical Athens
in Rome, thereby initiating what became known as
the Golden Age. The artistic style of the period was
characterized by a return to a sense of classical
timelessness and composure.

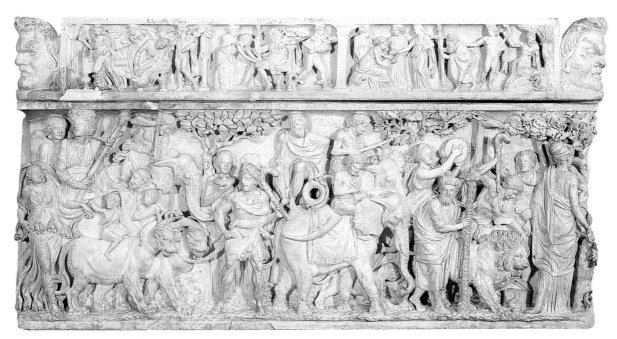

Sarcophagus with the Triumph of Dionysos
(Roman, later second century AD)
Marble, length 91 ins (221 cm)
Bequest of Henry Walters, 1931; 23.31

This sarcophagus was discovered in the underground
tomb of one of the most illustrious families in Roman
history (the Calpurnii Pisones). With its multiple
planes of figures, many worked almost in the round,
the monument exemplifies the masterful talents of
the Roman relief carvers. The triumphal march of
Dionysos through the lands of India was equated
in Roman thought with the triumph of the deceased
over death.

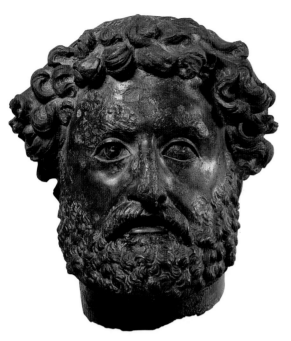

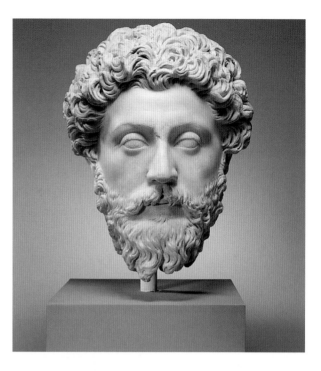

Private Portrait
(Roman, Antonine, c. 140-50 AD)
Bronze, height 11 ins (28.8 cm)
Bequest of Henry Walters, 1931; 23.66

The plastic curls at the forehead of this magnificent portrait are also seen on portraits of the Emperor Antoninus Pius (138-60 AD), but the thick locks over the crown of the head were characteristic under Hadrian (117-38 AD). Although the Empire still enjoyed prosperity during these years, troubled observers could already detect signs of its impending decline, and thus portraits often exhibit an unfocused sense of withdrawal that would be more noticeable in the art of succeeding decades.

Head of Marcus Aurelius
(Roman, 161-80 AD)
Marble, height 12 ⅝ ins (32 cm)
Bequest of Henry Walters, 1931; 23.215

From a noble Spanish family, Marcus Aurelius (121-80 AD) was selected when a youth to become emperor. His schooling in philosophy above all other disciplines resulted in his authorship of the celebrated *Meditations*. The beard and heavy eyelids bespeak the pensiveness of a conscientious ruler schooled in the Stoic values of purposefulness and self-denial.

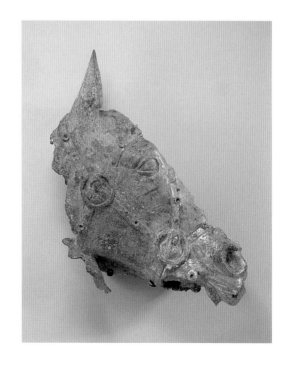

Horse Head
(Roman, first-second century AD)
Bronze, length 21 ½ ins (54.5cm)
Bequest of Henry Walters, 1931; 54.759

From a gilded equestrian monument, said to have been set up in northern Italy, this head enables us to envision the imposing and omnipresent public statuary that transmitted civic values to an admiring populace. The amount of bronze used in the head alone explains why most life-sized ancient bronze statuary was melted down for weaponary or implements in later moments of crisis.

Medieval Art

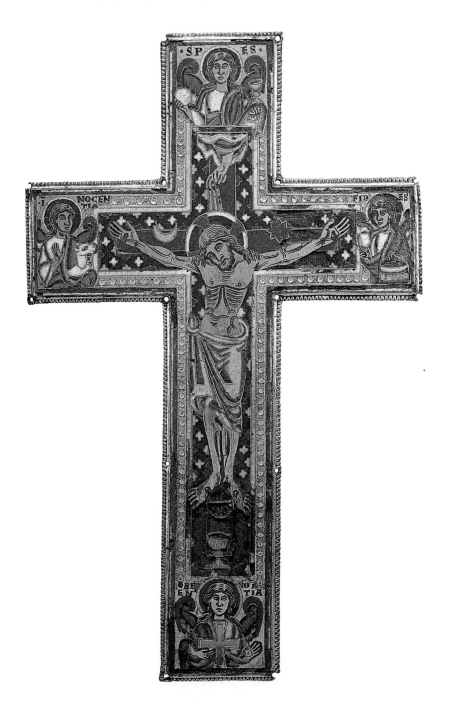

The "Rubens Vase"
(Early Byzantine, Constantinople (?), fourth century)
Agate and gold, height 7 ½ ins (19 cm)
Museum Purchase, 1941; 42.562

Carved in high relief from a single
piece of agate, this extraordinary vase,
ornamented with vine leaves and satyr
heads, was most likely created in an
imperial workshop for an early Byzantine
emperor. Since then the "Rubens Vase"
has passed through the hands of many
renowned collectors, including the dukes
of Anjou and King Charles V of France.
In 1619 it was purchased by the Flemish
painter Peter Paul Rubens (1577–1640),
after whom it is named. The vase
continued its travels through Europe,
to arrive finally in Baltimore in 1941.

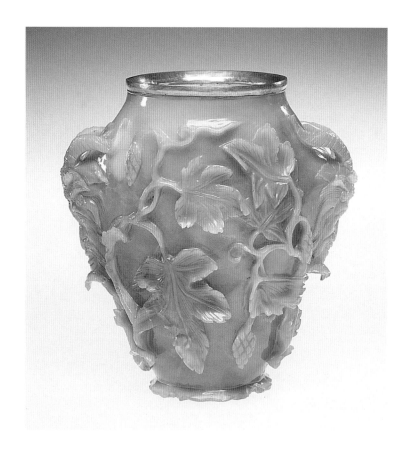

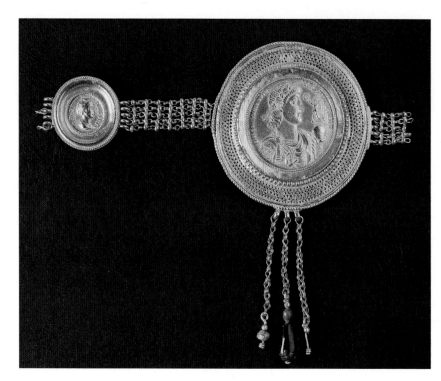

**Jewelry Section with Medallion
and Coin**
*(Early Byzantine, Constantinople (?),
later fourth century)*
Gold and semi-precious stones,
diameter of medallion 3 ¼ ins (8 cm),
length of section 7 ½ ins (19 cm)
Bequest of Henry Walters, 1931;
57.527 A,B

Imperial medallions, such as
this one of Constantius II (ruled
350-61), were often mounted
by their recipients to boast of
their highly favored status in
society. This stunning example,
minted in Nicomedia (Asia
Minor), represents on the reverse
the triumphant emperor in his
chariot. Smaller coins were also
mounted as jewelry, like this
aureus honoring Galeria Faustina
(died 140/1), wife of Antoninus
Pius. Other mounted coins,
separated by lengths of chain,
would have completed this
section of either a belt or a
necklace.

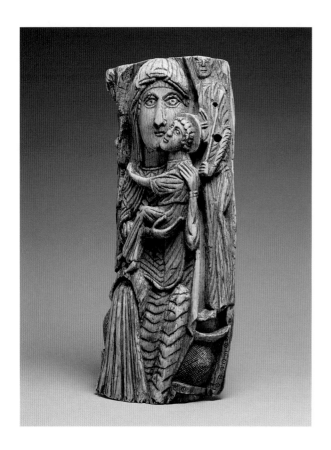

Ivory Relief of Virgin and Child
(Early Byzantine, Coptic Egypt, sixth-seventh century)
Ivory, 10 ¼ ins (26 cm)
Bequest of Henry Walters, 1931; 71.297

This unusually large ivory carving—whose curve
corresponds to the shape of the tusk—shows the
Christ Child embracing his mother in a pose of tender
intimacy. It is one of the earliest examples of what in
later Byzantine times was called Eleousa, or "Virgin of
Tenderness." The relief was likely to have been used
for private devotion, either in a monastic or domestic
setting, as a form of icon (Greek for "image"). Especially
striking, and typical of the early medieval period in
Christian Egypt, are the Virgin's large head, fixed gaze,
and angular drapery patterns.

Chalice with Apostles venerating the Cross
(Early Byzantine, Syria, early seventh century)
Silver, 6 ⅝ ins (16.9 cm)
Bequest of Henry Walters, 1931; 57.636

Encircling this graceful, arcaded
chalice are two pairs of apostles
flanking large crosses. The chalice is
one of twenty-three silver altar vessels
(formerly known as the "Hama
Treasure") believed to have been
found in the Syrian village of Kurin.
The Greek form of the name, Kaper
Koraon, is inscribed on the chalice.
The treasure was probably hidden in
the eighth century when, as a
consequence of Arab conquests, parts
of Syria were gradually abandoned by
Byzantine Christians. The altar vessels
form part of The Walters rich holdings
in Byzantine silver.

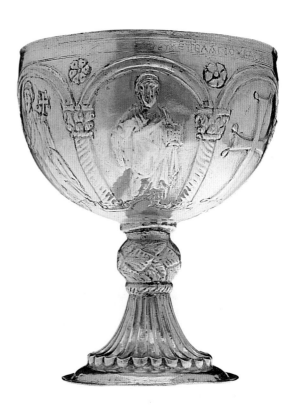

**Bookcover Plaque with Crucifixion
and the Three Marys at the Tomb**
(Carolingian, northern France, 870-80)
Ivory, height 6 ⁷⁄₁₆ ins (16.3 cm)
Bequest of Henry Walters, 1931; 71.142

To one side of Christ, crucified on a rough-hewn cross, are
the Virgin and the Roman solider Longinus with the lance;
on the other are St. John and Stephaton with the sponge.
The coiled serpent at the foot of the cross symbolizes the
conquered Devil. In the scene below, the three Marys are
greeted by the angel at the elaborate, empty tomb of Christ,
a three-tiered interpretation of the Holy Sepulcher in Jerusalem.
The style of the plaque, once placed on the cover of a Gospel
book, is characterized by animated figures, fluid drapery, and
rich, foliate borders.

Pair of Eagle Fibulae
(Visigothic Spain, sixth century)
Gold over bronze, semi-precious stones, meerschaum,
length 5 ¹¹⁄₁₆ ins (14.5 cm)
Bequest of Henry Walters, 1931; 54.421-422

This superb pair of eagle-shaped *fibulae*, found at Tierra de
Barros (Badajoz, southwest Spain), is made of sheet gold
over bronze inlaid with garnets, amethysts, and colored
glass. Similar *fibulae* have been excavated from Visigothic
graves in Spain and Ostrogothic graves in northern Italy
(the sites of their respective, sixth-century kingdoms),
but this pair is among the finest, being especially noted
for strong color and fluid lines. They would have been
worn at the same time to fasten a cloak at either shoulder,
and pendants once dangled from the loops at the bottom.

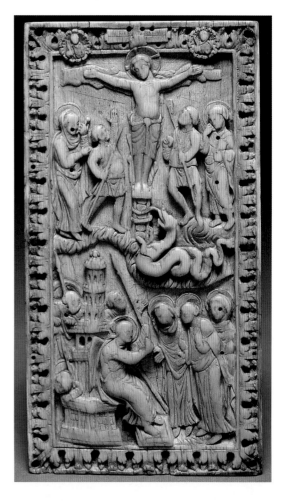

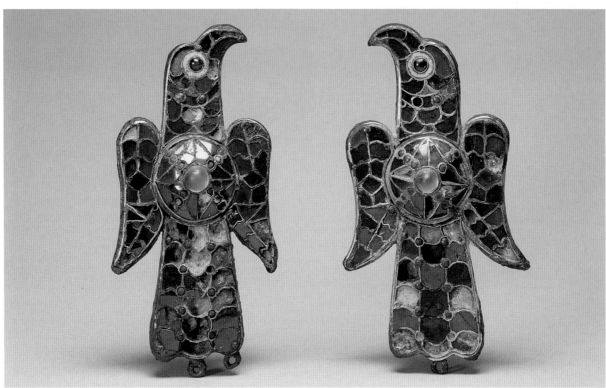

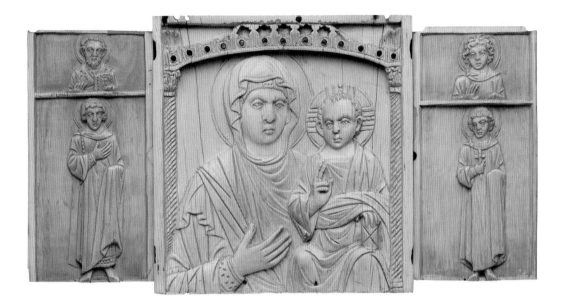

Triptych Icon of Hodegetria with Saints
(Byzantine, Constantinople, later tenth century)
Ivory, 4 ¾ x 9 ins (12 cm x 22.8 cm)
Bequest of Henry Walters, 1931; 71.158

The compositon is known as a Hodegetria, Greek for "She who shows the way," as the Virgin with her right hand indicates the Savior, the Child in her left arm.

The pose derives from the famous icon popularly thought to have been painted from life by St. Luke, and preserved in the Hodegon Monastery in Constantinople. On the wings are two pairs of unidentified saints, in bust- and full-length, who pay homage to the Virgin and Child. The fine carving of this triptych (three-panelled icon) has been worn down over time, a testament to its continued use and veneration.

Tile Icon of St. Nicholas
(Byzantine, Constantinople, tenth-eleventh century)
Glazed ceramic, 6 ⅝ x 6 ⁷⁄₁₆ ins (16.8 x 16.4 cm)
Museum Purchase, 1956; 48.2086.1

Framed by vine scrolls, St. Nicholas holds the Gospels with his covered left hand (a sign of respect), and raises his right in blessing. This ceramic tile is one of the finest in The Walters collection, which includes over 1,000 fragments, the largest group outside of Istanbul, Turkey. Although of unknown origin, they are similar to ones known to have been made in Constantinople. The tiles were most likely attached to a church wall as part of a series made up of saints and decorative, non-iconic pieces.

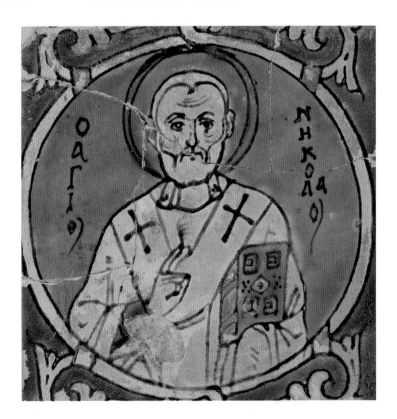

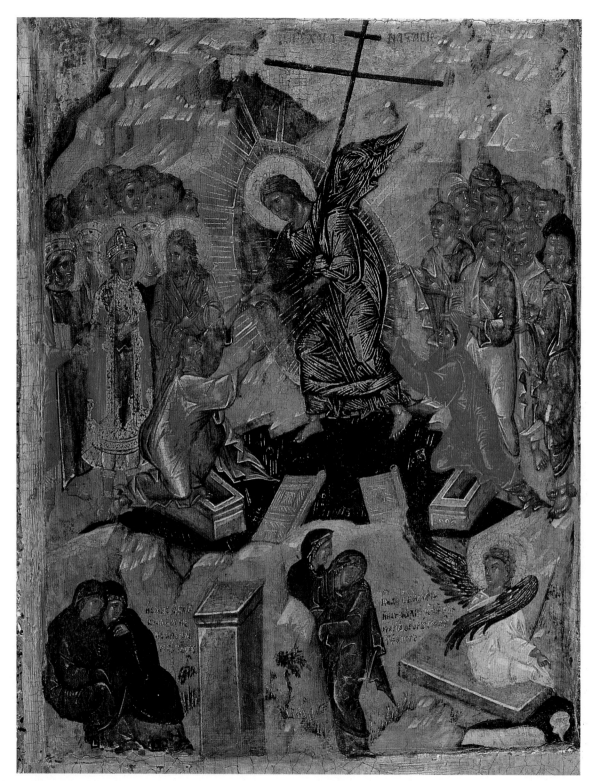

Icon of the Anastasis
(Byzantine, Macedonia, third quarter of the fourteenth century)
Tempera on wood, 14 ⁵⁄₁₆ x 10 ⁷⁄₁₆ ins (36 x 26.5 cm)
Bequest of Henry Walters, 1931; 37.751

The Anastasis is the Byzantine equivalent of that part
of the Resurrection in which Christ descends into
Hell (the Harrowing of Hell) to free the Just of the
Old Testament. Here Christ leans forward to draw
Adam from his tomb, while the rest of the Just,
including Eve at the right, wait their turn. In the
scenes below, the two Marys approach the empty
tomb of Christ, while at the right an angel announces
the Resurrection. One of the finest early icons in
America, this panel is remarkable for its delicate,
linear style and narrative complexity.

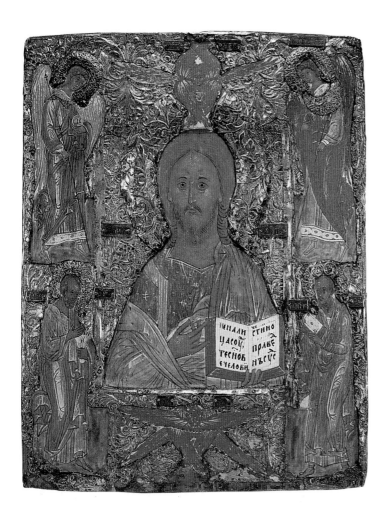

Icon of Christ
(Russian, Moscow, sixteenth century)
Tempera on wood and gilt silver,
11 ¾ x 9 ¼ ins (29.9 x 23.5 cm)
Bequest of Henry Walters, 1931; 37.1065B

Christ, seen in the pose of the Just Judge, holds a Gospel book open to John 7:24: "Judge not according to appearance...." Above and below are bright red seraphim, while at the sides are the venerating figures of Sts. Peter, Paul, and two archangels. Surrounding them is a rich, gilt silver revetment (known as *oklad*: cover), densely patterned with scrolls and leaves. This vividly colored icon forms the center of a Deësis, an arrangement in which the figure of Christ is flanked by panels of the Virgin on the left and John the Baptist on the right.

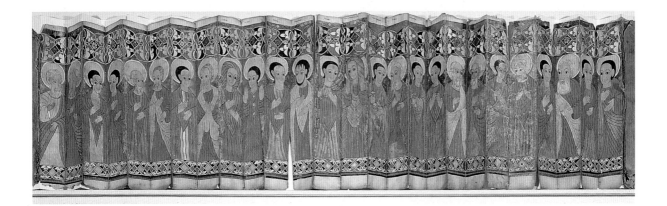

Liturgical Fan
(Ethiopian, late fifteenth century)
Parchment and tempera, 24 x 38 ½ ins (60 x 98 cm)
Museum Purchase through the W. Alton Jones Foundation Acquisition Fund, 1996; 36.9

This stunning fan, seen here spread horizontally, would normally be opened with the two ends held together to form a full circle. When thus arrayed, the central figure of Mary appears at the top surrounded by archangels, apostles, and prophets. Most striking in the painted fans and icons of Ethiopia is the use of bright, vivid colors, the large eyes of the figures, and the parallel patterns of the drapery. This rare fan exemplifies the "Gunda Gunde Style" of manuscript decoration as it developed in the late fifteenth and early sixteenth centuries.

**End of a Reliquary Shrine with Christ
Trampling the Beasts**
(Mosan, late eleventh and thirteenth centuries)
Silver, silver gilt, horn and *champlevé* enamel,
height 23 ⅟₁₆ ins (58.5 cm)
Bequest of Henry Walters, 1931; 57.519

Psalm 91:13 is the source for this silver panel: "Thou shall
tread upon the lion and the adder: the young lion and the
dragon shalt thou trample under feet." Both the dragon, seen
here as a winged, fish-tailed serpent, and the lion symbolize
the evil that is conquered by Christ. Surrounding the scene is
a thirteenth-century frame containing relics of saints in small
compartments of translucent horn. The entire panel is one end
of the lost reliquary of St. Oda of Amay (Belgium), the other
end of which is in the British Museum, London.

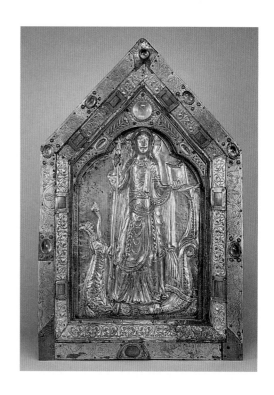

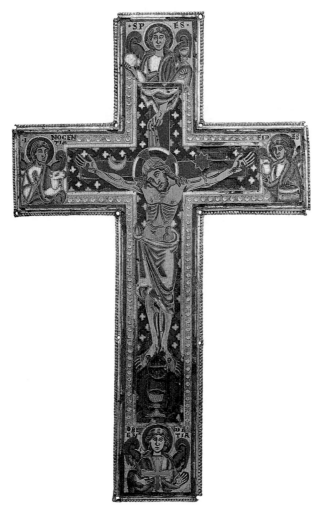

Reliquary Cross
(Mosan, mid-twelfth century)
Champlevé and *cloisonné* enamel,
height 11 ⅞₁₆ ins (29 cm)
Bequest of Henry Walters, 1931; 44.98

This is the front portion of a rare
enameled cross which is immediately
striking for its finely detailed figures
and subtle shades of enamel. Christ
is here surrounded by four Virtues
(top, clockwise): Hope (SPES) with the
Eucharistic bread and chalice; Faith
(FIDES) with a baptismal font; Obedience
(OBEDIENTIA) with a cross; and
Innocence (INNOCENTIA) holding a
lamb. Below Christ's feet a Eucharistic
chalice catches his blood. The cross was
once backed by a second panel to form a
reliquary, with a piece of the True Cross
placed in the cavity at the bottom.

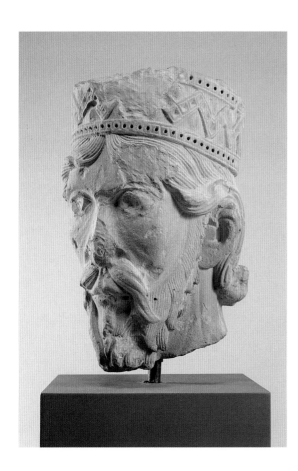

Head of an Old Testament King
(French, Saint-Denis, c. 1140)
Limestone, height 14 ⁹⁄₁₆ ins (36 cm)
Bequest of Henry Walters, 1931; 27.21

The severe Romanesque style has here begun to give way to the freer, more naturalistic elements of the Gothic, as seen in the "soft" modeling of the features and the waves and curls of the hair. Carved for the abbey church of Saint-Denis (just north of Paris), this dignified Old Testament king served as a model of secular rulership for the French kings who patronized this important church. The head, once part of a column figure on the west façade, was broken off during the French Revolution, when Saint-Denis became a target for vandalism.

Altar Frontal with the Life of St. Martin
(Spanish, Catalonia, 1201)
Tempera on panel and stucco, 41 ⅛ x 62 ⅛ ins (104.5 x 157.7 cm)
Bequest of Henry Walters, 1931; 37.1188

Surrounding the central figure of Christ in Majesty are scenes from the Life of St. Martin, which read *(clockwise from upper left)*: St. Martin cutting his cloak in half to share with a beggar; St. Martin's vision of Christ clothed in the cloak; the soul of St. Martin carried to heaven by angels; St. Martin ordained Bishop of Tours. The panel, dated 1201 by the fragmentary inscription at the lower left, once served as an *antependium*, or altar frontal, in a Catalan church in northeastern Spain.

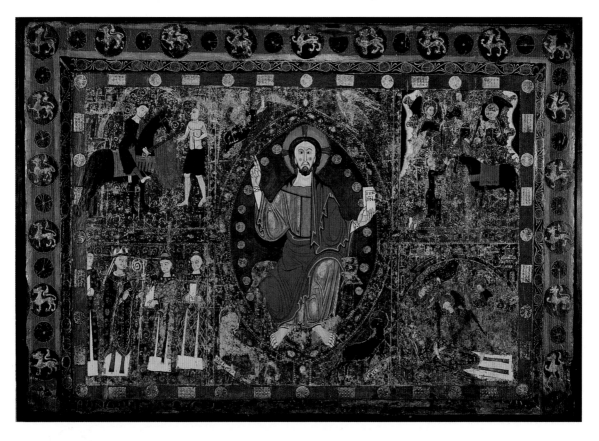

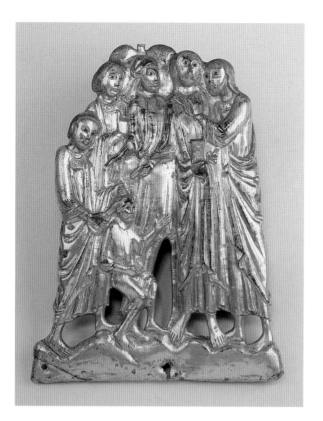

Relief Plaque of the Betrayal of Christ
(French, Limoges, mid-thirteenth century)
Copper gilt, 13 ¾ x 10 ⅝ ins (35 x 27 cm)
Bequest of Henry Walters, 1931; 53.10

This dramatic composition depicts the moment
when Christ is kissed by Judas and thus identified
for the Roman soldiers who have come to arrest him
(Matthew 26:47-52). At the left one of Christ's followers
prepares to cut off the ear of the high priest's servant,
an act which Christ condemns with the extension of
his hand. The elongated, Gothic figures with their
rhythmical drapery patterns form a tight, emotional
unit striking for its sense of the theatrical. The relief
is one of a series of the *Life of Christ* which once made
up an enameled altar panel.

Eucharistic Dove
(French, Limoges, early thirteenth century)
Champlevé enamel, glass, height 7 ins (17.8 cm)
Bequest of Henry Walters, 1931; 44.3

Used for storing communion wafers,
Eucharistic doves were suspended by
chains above the altar to signify the
presence of the Holy Spirit at the Mass.
In this particularly fine example the
sparkling eyes and shimmering enamels
of the wings and tail underscore the
material richness of the piece. The dove's
breast is incised with a diamond pattern
suggesting feathers, adding to the naturalistic
portrayal of the bird. The application of
enamel to curved pieces of metal is
extremely difficult, and here stands as
a testimonial to the skill of the Limoges
craftsmen.

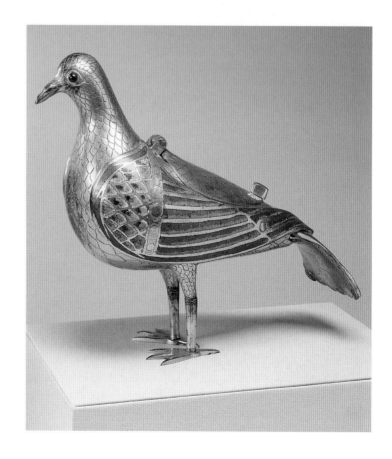

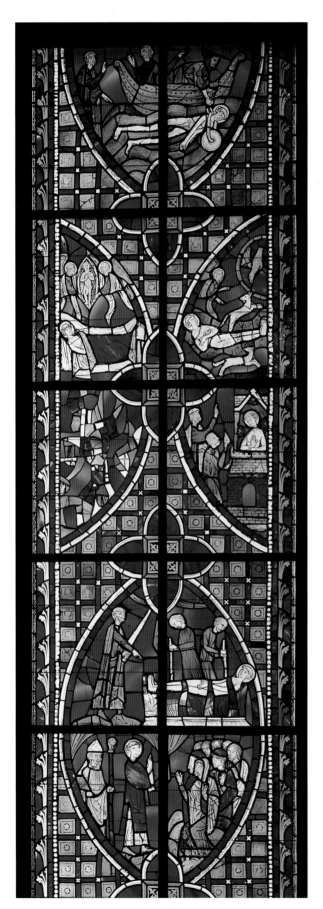

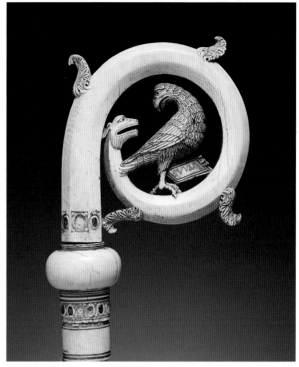

Crozier Head with Eagle of St. John
(Italian (?), thirteenth century)
Ivory and glass paste inlay, height 8 ins (20.3 cm)
Bequest of Henry Walters, 1931; 71.300

The head of this crozier, or bishop's staff of office,
is ornamented with bands of inlay on the shaft and
acanthus leaves along the curved volute, terminating
in the head of a dragon. The detailed and expressive
eagle, the symbol of St. John, holds in one claw a book
representing the Gospel. Traces of paint on the bird's
feathers and on the volute indicate that the crozier was
orginally polychromed and gilded. The piece has been
linked stylistically with a group of croziers from Sicily.

Refectory Window with the Life of St. Vincent
(French, Paris, mid-thirteenth century)
Stained and painted glass, 127 ¼ x 42 ins
(323.5 x 106.7 cm)
Bequest of Henry Walters, 1931; 46.65

This window was originally part of a series devoted
to the Life of St. Vincent in the refectory, or dining hall,
of the monastery of Saint-Germain-des-Prés, Paris. The
scenes, in glowing, jewel-tones, read *(from bottom to top)*:
Vincent preaching; Vincent tortured by fire; *(central
panels, bottom left, anticlockwise)*: a modern replacement;
Vincent in prison; Vincent's body protected from ravens
by foxes; Vincent's soul ascending to heaven; and
Vincent's body thrown into the sea. In showing the great
suffering this saint endured for his faith, the window set
an example for the monks who gazed upon it daily.

43

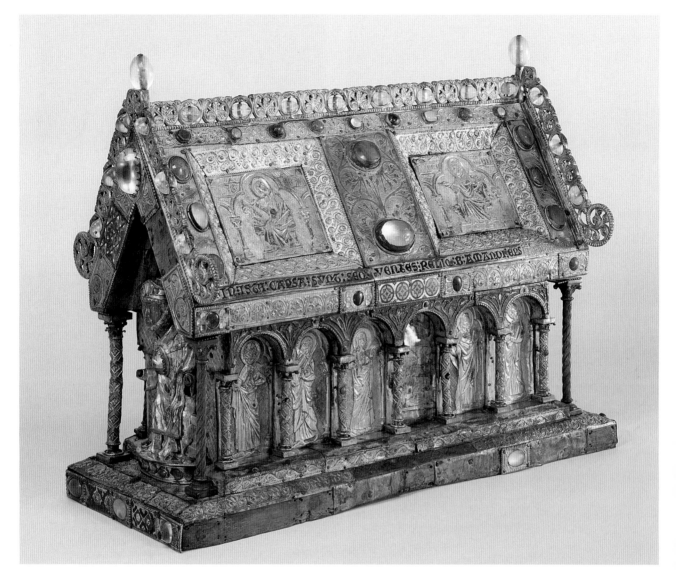

Reliquary Shrine of St. Amandus
(Flemish, 1250-75)
Copper gilt, silver, *champlevé* enamel, and semi-precious stones,
19 5/16 x 25 ins (49 x 63.5 cm)
Bequest of Henry Walters, 1931; 53.9

This shrine once housed the relics of St. Amandus, a
seventh-century missionary to the French and Flemish
regions. Its shape suggests a small church with a gabled,
crested roof supported by an arcade of slender, silver
columns. Along the sides are standing figures of apostles,
and on the roof are plaques of the four Evangelists. The
seated figure on one end may represent St. Amandus.
Shrines such as this played an important role in the life
of a church, forming the focal point of pilgrimage,
prayers for miracles, and processions on holy days.

Helmet (Sallet) with Visor
(German, c. 1490)
Iron and steel, 9 ⅛ x 15 ½ ins (23 x 39.5 cm)
Bequest of Henry Walters, 1931; 51.470

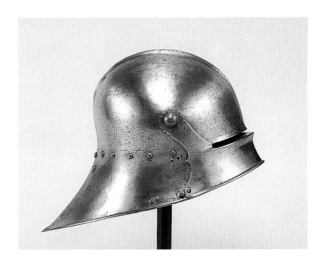

The characteristic German battle helmet of the later Middle Ages—the long-tailed sallet—was both a work of art and a triumph of technology. Designed for a knight on horseback, the helmet is composed of an outer shell of steel to resist penetration and an inner shell of iron to prevent shattering. Its smooth, flowing profile could deflect even the most formidable blows from maces, swords, and crossbow bolts.

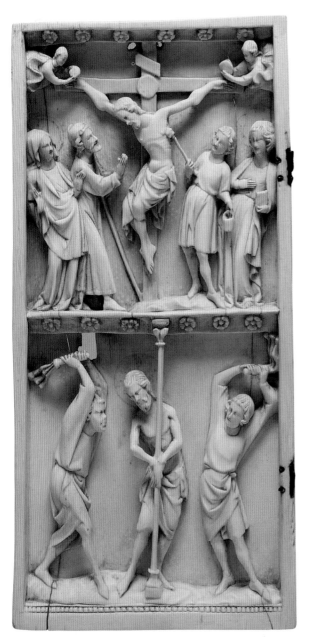

Diptych Leaf of Crucifixion and Flagellation
(French, Paris, first quarter of the fourteenth century)
Ivory, 8 ¾ x 4 ³⁄₁₆ ins (22.2 x 10.6 cm)
Bequest of Henry Walters, 1931; 71.124

Bands of small roses placed at the top of the two scenes identify this plaque as one of the "Rose Group" of ivories, characterized by their carefully arranged figures and graceful poses. The upper register shows the Crucifixion, with Christ accompanied by Mary and the Roman soldier Longinus (*left*) and Stephaton, the sponge-bearer, and St. John (*right*). Below is the scene of the Flagellation, noteworthy for the curved, almost mannered poses of the figures ("Gothic sway"). The original program of this devotional diptych was complemented by the Deposition and Entombment on the right leaf.

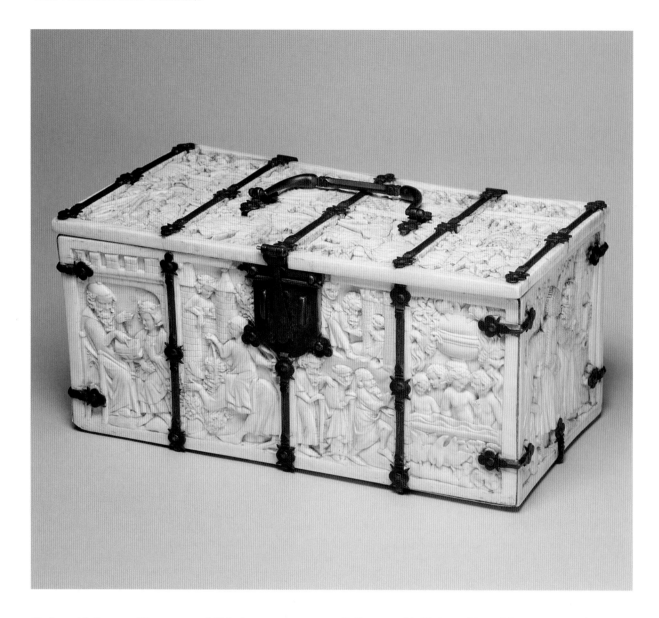

Casket with Scenes of Romance and Chivalry
(French, Paris, c. 1330-50)
Ivory, with modern iron mounts, 4 ½ x 9 ¹¹⁄₁₆ ins
(11.5 x 24.6 cm)
Bequest of Henry Walters, 1931; 71.264

This splendid casket, perhaps once used as a jewel box,
is carved with scenes from romances and allegorical
literature representing the courtly ideals of love and
heroism. In the center of the lid knights joust as ladies
watch from a balcony; to the left, knights lay siege to
the Castle of Love, and to the right a knight and a lady
engage in a mock joust, armed with bunches of flowers
and foliage. The remaining scenes on the casket are
drawn from stories about Aristotle and Phyllis, Tristan
and Iseult, and tales of the heroic deeds of Gawain,
Galahad, and Lancelot.

Reliquary with Christ as Man of Sorrows (opposite)
(Bohemian, Prague, 1347-49)
Silver gilt, enamel, and semi-precious stones,
height 11 ¹³⁄₁₆ ins (30 cm)
Bequest of Henry Walters, 1931; 57.700

On this striking reliquary Christ is surrounded by the
instruments of his Passion: the cross, the hammer and
nails, and the scourge and whips. At his feet are the dice
thrown by the soldiers who cast lots for his garments,
and beside them a tiny angel holds a gabled niche which
originally housed a relic from the Crown of Thorns.
On the base of this unique reliquary are four shields
representing Czech and German territories ruled by the
Holy Roman Emperor Charles IV in 1347-49, and an
inscription refering to the donor as John Volek, Bishop
of Olmütz (1334-51), in the region east of Bohemia.

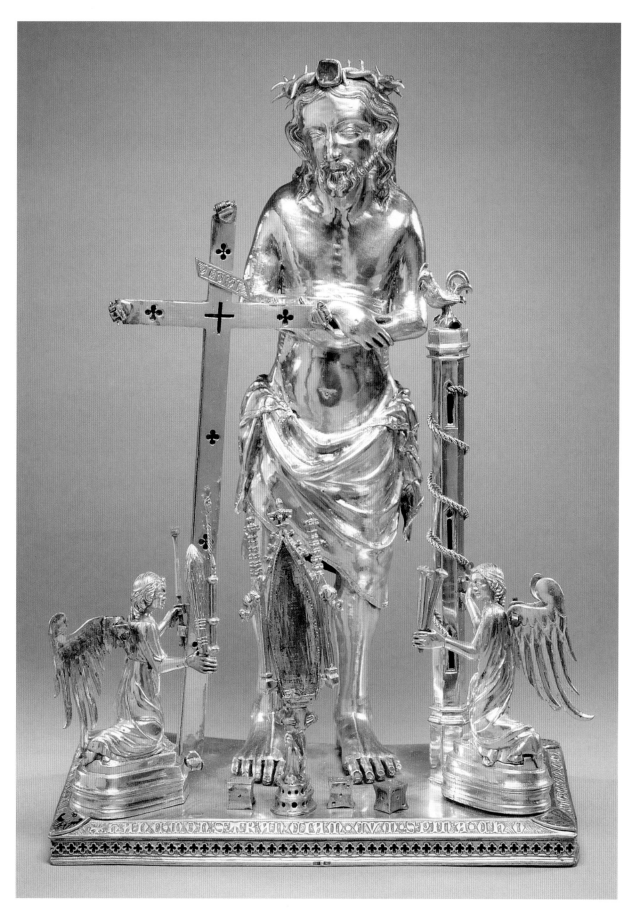

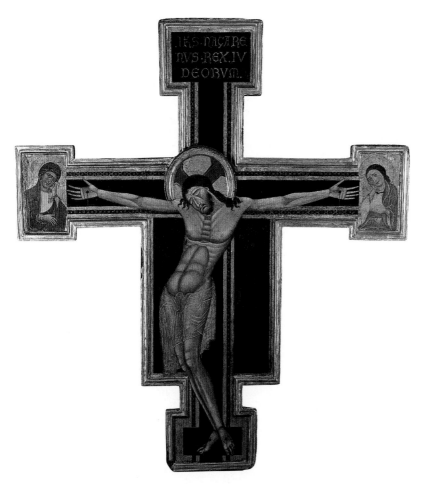

Crucifix
(Italian, Florence, late thirteenth century)
Tempera and gold leaf on panel,
98 ¹¹⁄₁₆ x 89 ⁹⁄₁₆ ins (250.7 x 227.5 cm)
Bequest of Henry Walters, 1931; 37.710

A potent symbol of sacrifice, Christ
is isolated against a dark background
and flanked by the grieving Virgin
and St. John. His sagging torso and
deeply etched face emphasize his
human pain, striking a similar
emotional chord to that which
resonates from Byzantine icons of
the twelfth century. The eloquent
curves of his body form a majestic
rhythm, while the rich reds and
gold leaf suggest the splendor of the
Kingdom of Heaven. This crucifix,
in the style of the Florentine master
Cimabue (c. 1240–c. 1302), is one of
the masterpieces of The Walters
collection of early Italian paintings.

Naddo Ceccarelli
(Italian, Siena, active mid-fourteenth century)
Madonna and Child
Tempera and gold leaf on panel,
24 ⁷⁄₁₆ x 17 ⅛ ins (62 x 43.5 cm)
Bequest of Henry Walters, 1931; 37.1159

An image of the standing Virgin and Child is set into the
front of a reliquary with two spires and a Gothic gabled
top ornamented with small, hook-shaped crockets. The
frame contains, within glass-covered roundels, a number
of saints' relics accompanied by small handwritten notes
recording their origins and significance. The back of the
panel is decorated with a painted marble design, which
adds to the precious nature of this jewel-like work. The
entire pane is supported by a freestanding base which
suggests that the reliquary once stood upon an altar.

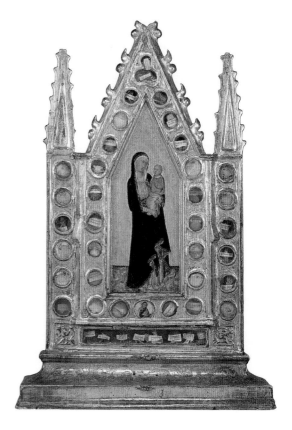

Renaissance & Baroque Art

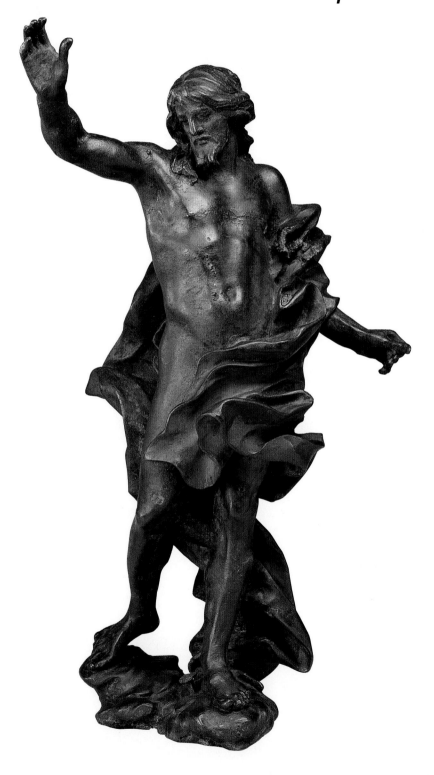

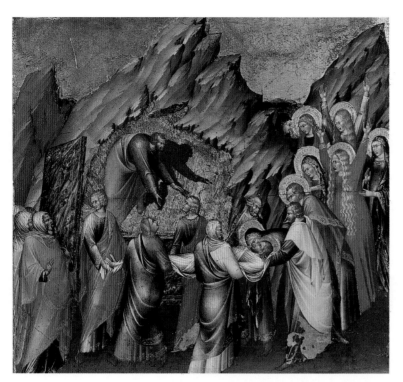

Giovanni di Paolo
(Italian, Siena, active 1420-82)
The Entombment, 1426
Tempera and gold leaf on panel,
15⅞ x 17 1/16 ins (40.3 x 43.3 cm)
Bequest of Henry Walters, 1931; 37.489 D

This is one of four panels from the predella or base section of a polyptych altarpiece featuring the Madonna and Child and saints, formerly in the church of San Domenico in Siena. The four Walters panels depict scenes from the life of Christ. While the graceful Entombment is characteristic of the Sienese school, the naturalistic shadow cast by the figure of Nicodemus who stoops to receive the body of Christ is extraordinary and possibly the earliest representation of a shadow in Italian Renaissance art.

Bicci di Lorenzo and Stefano di Antonio
(Italian, Florence, 1373-1452 and 1407-83)
The Annunciation, c. 1430
Tempera and gold leaf on panel,
64 ¾ x 56 15/16 ins (164.4 x 144.7 cm)
Bequest of Henry Walters, 1931; 37.448

A remarkably preserved complete altarpiece, with predella, frame, and canopy, *The Annunciation* is complemented by the smaller predella paintings of the birth of the Virgin, her presentation in the temple, and death. While the elegance of *The Annunciation*, with its subtle organization of spaces and graceful flow of drapery, attests to Bicci di Lorenzo's authorship, the predella was painted by the master's assistant Stefano di Antonio.

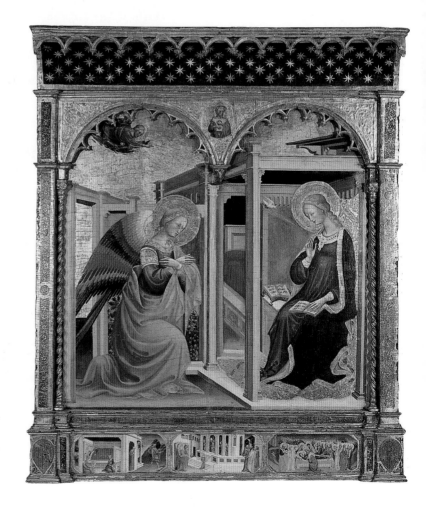

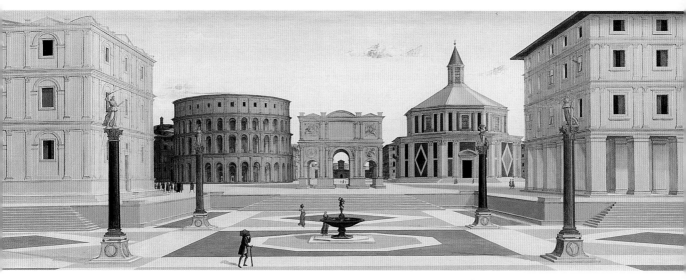

Unknown Central Italian artist
(active c. 1490-1505)
View of an Ideal City, c. 1490-1500
Oil on panel, 31 ⅝ x 86 ⅚ ins (80.3 x 219.8 cm)
Bequest of Henry Walters, 1931; 37.677

Based on a thoughtful exploration of one-point perspective, this panel by an unidentified artist exemplifies Renaissance principles of urban planning.

The buildings, including the Roman Colosseum, the Florentine Baptistery, and a triumphal arch, are incorporated into an imaginary city-scape and represent three main aspects of communal life: military, recreational, spiritual. The whole composition can thus be seen as an allegory of the well-ordered, ideal city. This painting and two similar panels in the Galleria Nazionale delle Marche, Urbino, and the Staatliche Museen, Gemäldegalerie, Berlin, were most likely originally inserted into the wainscot of a room.

Rafaello Sanzio, called Raphael, and workshop
(Italian, Umbria, 1483-1520)
Madonna of the Candelabra, 1513-14
Oil on panel, 25 ³⁄₁₆ x 25 ⅞ ins
(64 x 65.7 cm)
Bequest of Henry Walters, 1931; 37.484

When purchased by Henry Walters in 1900, this painting became the first Raphael *Madonna* to enter an American collection. A seventeenth-century inventory indicates that the original panel also included St. John the Baptist. It is to the young Baptist who once appeared in the lower right of the painting that the Madonna's downcast gaze would have been directed.

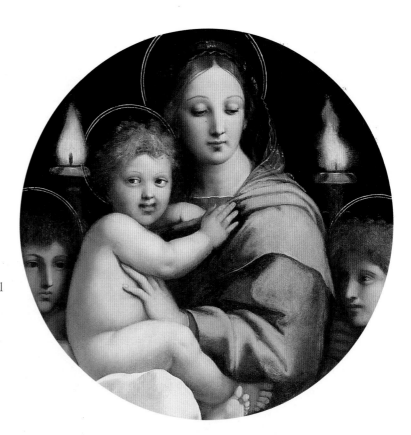

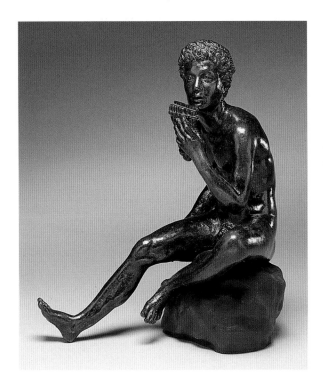

Andrea Briosco, called Riccio
(Italian, Padua, c. 1470-1532)
The Shepherd Daphnis, 1515-20
Bronze, height 8 ⅜ ins (21.3 cm)
Bequest of Henry Walters, 1931; 54.234

Riccio was a member of the humanist circles at Padua,
a famous university city, and there studied antiquities
collected by local scholars. He never directly copied
ancient sculptures however, and instead masterfully
conveyed their spirit. In *The Shepherd Daphnis* Riccio
recreated the pastoral mood of classical sculpture.

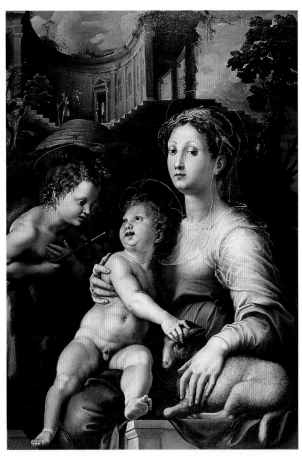

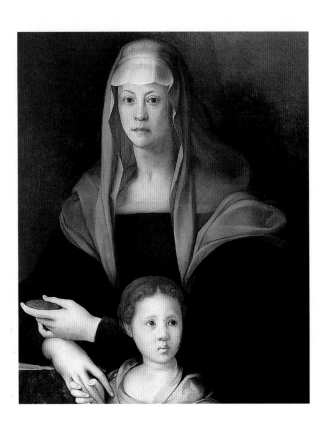

Jacopo Carucci, called Pontormo
(Italian, Florence, 1494-1556)
**Portrait of Maria Salviati with a Little Girl (probably
Giulia de'Medici), 1539-40**
Oil on panel, 34 ⅝ x 28 ⅟₁₆ ins (88 x 71.3 cm)
Bequest of Henry Walters, 1931; 37.596

Maria Salviati was a member of the powerful Medici
family and the wife of a famous military leader Giovanni
delle Bande Nere (died 1526). The little girl holding her
hand is probably Giulia, who was in Maria's care after
the murder of her father, Duke Alessandro de'Medici
(1511-37). Though Maria wears simple clothing as a
sign of mourning for her deceased husband, the
portrait conveys aristocratic refinement intensified
by Pontormo's elegant style, especially noticeable
in the sitter's impossibly long and boneless fingers.

Giulio Romano and workshop (opposite)
(Italian, Rome, 1499-1546)
The Madonna and Child
with St. John the Baptist, mid-1520s
Oil on panel, 49 ½ x 33 ⅝ ins (125.7 x 85.4 cm)
Bequest of Henry Walters, 1931; 37.548

The most gifted of Raphael's students, Giulio Romano
imbued his figures with the statuesque dignity
characteristic of his master. At the same time, Giulio was
fascinated with the new tendencies toward elongation
and fantastic architecture. The fanciful structure seen in
the background may derive from the now-vanished
exedra erected by Donate Bramante (1444-1514) in the
Vatican gardens. Until 1989 the painting was attributed
to Raffaello dal Colle (1490-1566), an artist who worked
under both Raphael (1483-1520) and Giulio Romano.

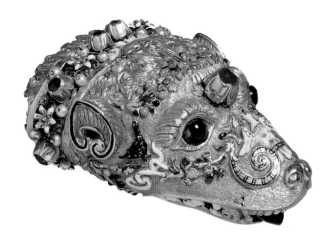

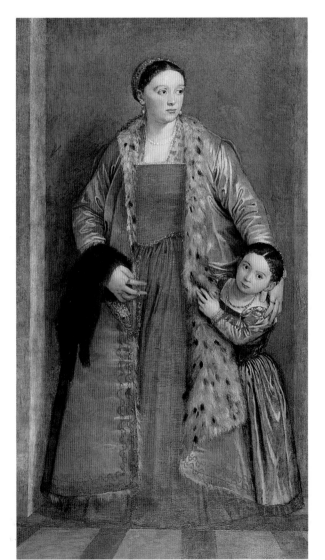

Unknown Italian artist
(Venice, sixteenth century)
Marten's Head, 1550-60
Enameled gold, ruby, garnets, and pearls,
height 3 ⁵⁄₁₆ ins (8.4 cm)
Acquired through exchange, 1967; 57.1982

A jeweled head similar to this is attached to a marten's
pelt held by Countess da Porto in Veronese's portrait
(left). The marten was thought to conceive its young
through its ears, free from sexual intercourse, and was
thus a symbol of Christ's miraculous conception. This
symbolic meaning is indicated by the presence of the
dove of the Incarnation on the creature's snout. Such
objects were fashionable in Europe during the sixteenth
century. They also served as protective amulets for
pregnant women.

Paolo Caliari, called Paolo Veronese
(Italian, Venice, 1528-88)
Portrait of Countess Livia da Porto Thiene
and her Daughter, Porzia, c. 1551
Oil on canvas, 82 ¹⁄₁₆ x 47 ⅝ ins (208.4 x 121 cm)
Bequest of Henry Walters, 1931; 37.541

This full-length portrait of the Countess da Porto and her
daughter shows Veronese's mastery of a new painting
format. It accompanied a portrait of the Countess's
husband, Count Giuseppe da Porto, and their eldest
son, Adriano (now in Palazzo Pitti, Florence). Thus it is
toward her husband, one of the most influential men in
Vicenza, that the Countess directs her glance. The couple
had five more children, and Livia is probably pregnant
here. Her fingers point to her stomach, and she holds a
fur of a marten, an animal which in the Renaissance was
believed to protect women in childbirth.

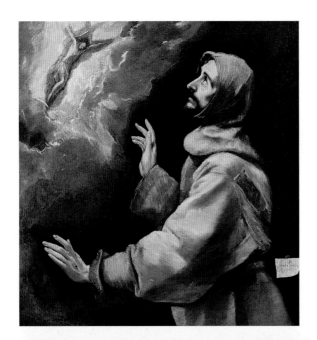

Domenikos Theotokopulos, called El Greco
(Greek, worked in Spain, 1541-1614)
St. Francis Receiving the Stigmata, c. 1585-90
Oil on canvas (transfered from original canvas),
40 ³/₁₆ x 38 ³/₁₆ ins (102 x 97 cm)
Bequest of Henry Walters, 1931; 37.424

This miraculous vision of the crucified Christ experienced by St. Francis was a favorite subject of El Greco. The artist, himself a lay Franciscan, has masterfully captured the transfixed state of the saint and created a quintessential expression of the mystical and emotional spirituality of the contemporary Counter-Reformation movement.

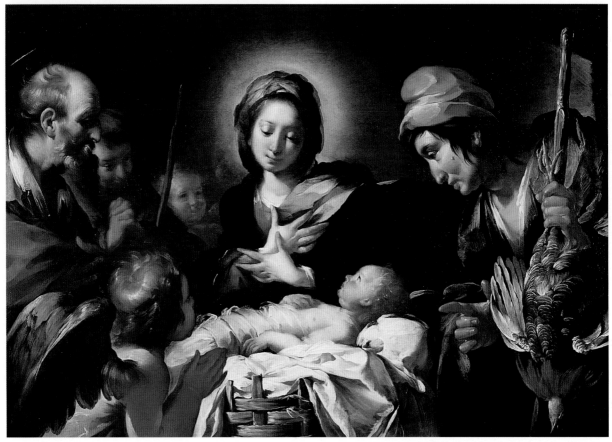

Bernardo Strozzi
(Italian, Genoa, 1581/2-1644)
Adoration of the Shepherds, c. 1618
Oil on canvas, 38 ½ x 54 ⅞ ins (97.8 x 139.4 cm)
Bequest of Henry Walters, 1931; 37.277

Strozzi, a master of the Italian Baroque, had been a Capuchin friar for ten years. In this intimate scene, both the emphasis on the humble circumstances of Christ's birth and the palpable realism with which the figures are painted accord with the spirit of the Counter-Reformation, which encouraged ideals of poverty and simplicity, as well as the use of both imagination and the senses in meditation on Christ's life.

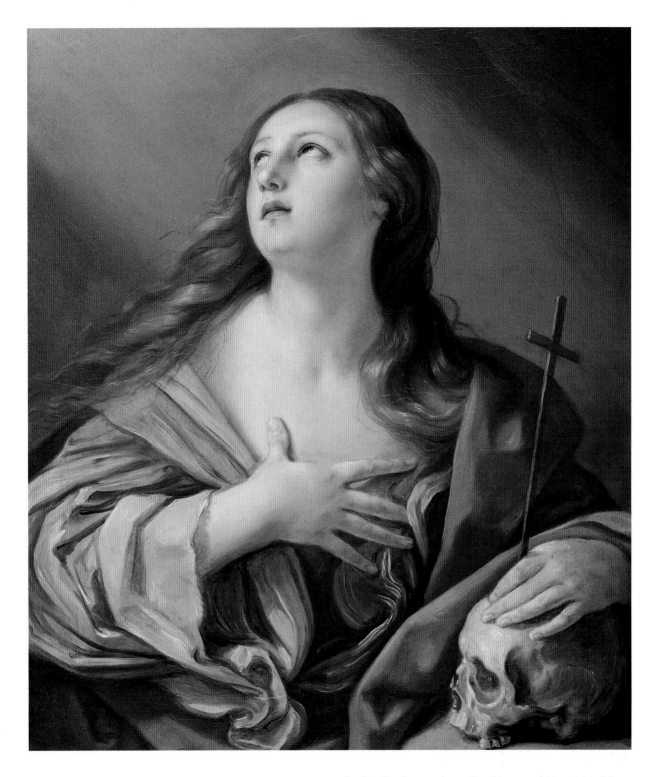

Guido Reni
(Italian, Bologna, 1575-1642)
The Penitent Magdalene, c. 1638
Oil on canvas, 35 ¾ x 29 ¼ ins (90.8 x 74.3 cm)
Museum Purchase through the W. Alton Jones Foundation
Acquisition Fund and The Walters Acquisition Fund,
1987; 37.2631

In this flamboyant but refined image of Mary Magdalen
created by the foremost Baroque master of the school
of Bologna, the converted sinner raises her eyes toward
heaven as she is illuminated by a stream of divine light.
Images of female saints who could be depicted in a
seductive manner were very popular with some artists
and patrons in the seventeenth century, and Reni painted
many versions of this composition.

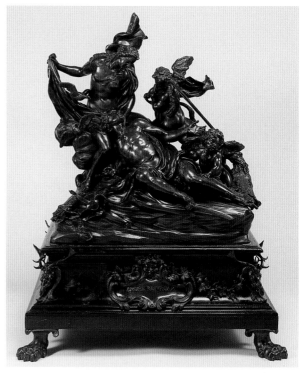

Massimiliano Soldani Benzi
(Italian, Florence, 1658-1740)
Adonis Mourned by Venus and Putti, 1729
Bronze, height 18 ½ ins (47 cm)
Bequest of Henry Walters, 1931; 54.677

Soldani was a master of the mint at the Medici court
in Florence and started his artistic career as a medalist.
The elegant drama unfolding before the viewer's
eyes exhibits the flamboyant, pictorial qualities of
Soldani's late-Baroque style. The romantic subject,
high degree of craftsmanship inviting close inspection,
and relatively small size suggest that this masterpiece
was intended as a collector's piece.

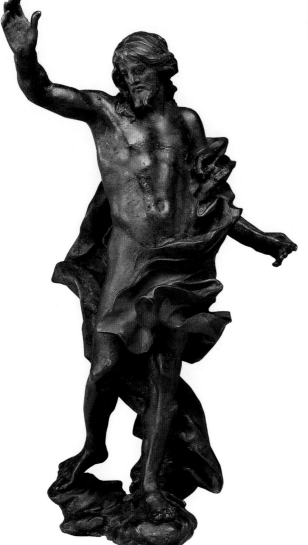

Gian Lorenzo Bernini
(Italian, Rome, 1598-1680)
The Risen Christ, 1673-4
Bronze, height 17 ⁵⁄₁₆ ins (44 cm)
Gift of C. Morgan Marshall, 1942; 54.2281

In 1673 Bernini was commissioned by Pope Clement X
(1670-76) to design a tabernacle crowned with the
figures of the twelve apostles and the Risen Christ
for the altar of the Chapel of the Blessed Sacrament in
St. Peter's, Rome. The Walters figure was an early cast
that was apparently set aside because of the crack
running across the chest. Another statuette was
successfully cast, gilded, and set atop the tabernacle,
where it remains to this day. Gazing down at the
worshippers, the dynamic figure clad in swirling
drapery embodies Christ's triumph over death.

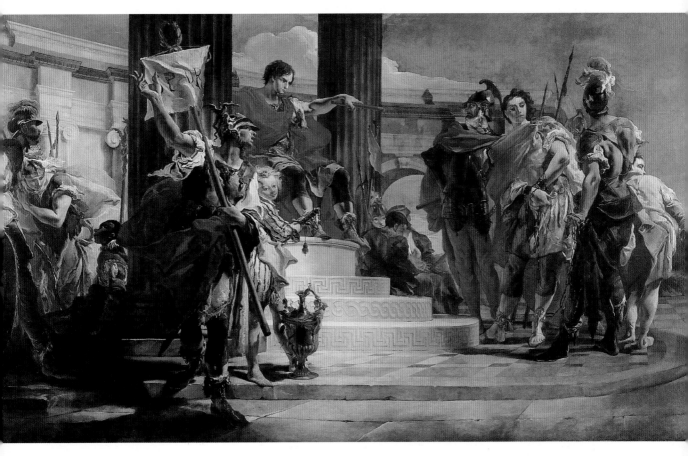

Giovanni Battista Tiepolo
(Italian, Venice, 1696-1770)
Scipio Africanus Freeing Massiva, c. 1720
Oil on canvas (transfered from original canvas),
110 x 191 ¹⁵/₁₆ ins (279.4 x 487.6 cm)
Bequest of Henry Walters, 1931; 37.657

In this early masterpiece Tiepolo combines dramatic gesture, grand scale, and classical architecture to create an image of generosity and statesmanship that was well suited to adorn the walls of a patrician palace in Venice. The subject has been identified as an episode from the life of Scipio Africanus, a Roman general of the late third century BC whose statesmanship and foreign conquests made him a popular subject for monumental painting in seventeenth-century Venice.

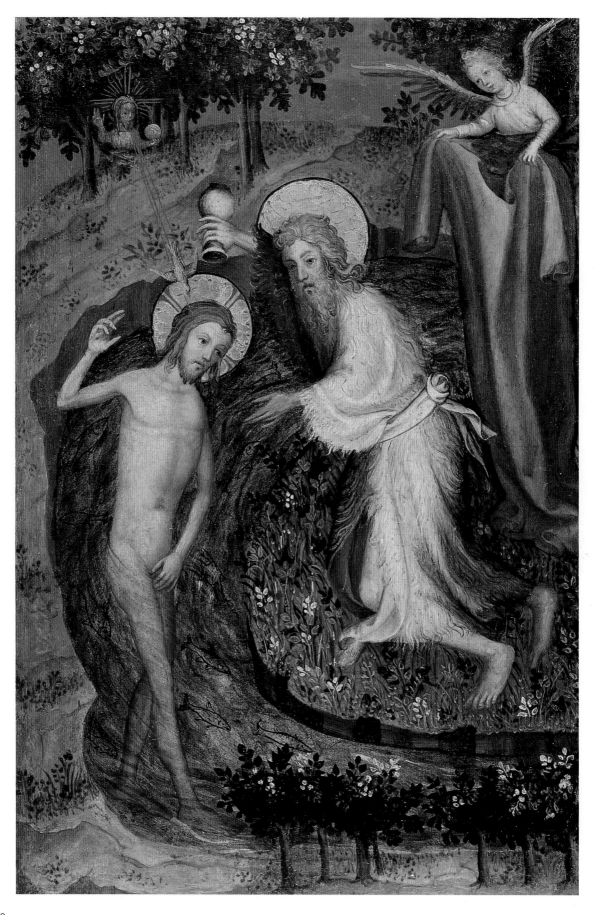

The Baptism of Christ (opposite)
(Netherlandish, c. 1400)
Oil (and tempera?) with gold leaf on panel,
14 ¹³⁄₁₆ x 10 ⁵⁄₁₆ ins (38 x 26.5 cm)
Purchased from Mrs. Henry Walters, 1939; 37.1683 B

This *Baptism* is an outer wing of a small, folding
altarpiece of which one half (including the *Annunciation*
and *Calvary*) belongs to The Walters and the other (the
Nativity, Resurrection, St. Christopher) to the Museum
Meyer van den Bergh, Antwerp. The entire, splendid
altarpiece can be traced back to the Carthusian
monastery of Champmol near Dijon, France, founded
by Philip the Bold (1342-1404), Duke of Burgundy,
and surely was made for Philip to take on his travels.
Charming details, such as fish swimming in the stream,
reveal the unknown artist's delight in naturalistic
representation. Tests indicate that these panels are
among the earliest to have been painted using oil.

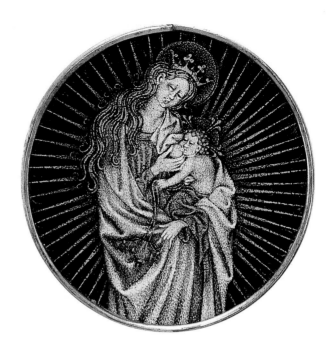

Medallion with the Emperor Augustus' Vision of the Virgin and Child
(Franco-Flemish, c. 1420)
Silver, gilt, enamel, diameter 2 ¹⁄₁₆ ins (5.2 cm)
Bequest of Henry Walters, 1931; 44.462

This miniature pendant is one of the earliest and finest
surviving examples of painted enamel. It is probably
connected to the jewelry and illuminated manuscripts
produced and collected at the court of John, Duke of
Berry (1340-1416), where artists often combined the
skills of goldsmithing and manuscript illumination. The
medallion is decorated on both sides, with Emperor
Augustus appearing on reverse.

Madonna of the Inkpot
(Franco-Flemish, c. 1415)
Oil and gold leaf on panel with engaged frame,
8 ¾ ins (22.3 cm)
Museum Purchase, 1964; 37.2404

The combination of complex iconography,
naturalistic details, and delicate execution in
this work is characteristic of the International
Gothic style that flourished during the early fifteenth
century. The painting derives its round shape from
contemporary convex mirrors, and was probably
intended to hang at the head of a bed. One of a few
small circular panels surviving from the period, it
presents the Virgin, humanity's intercessor before
Christ, holding a tiny inkpot in which the Christ
Child is about to dip his pen before inscribing the
names of the saved and the damned.

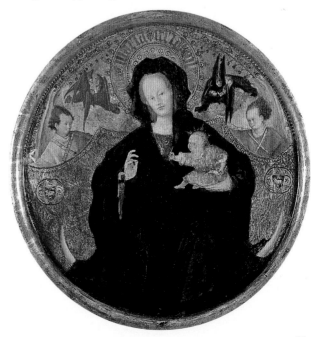

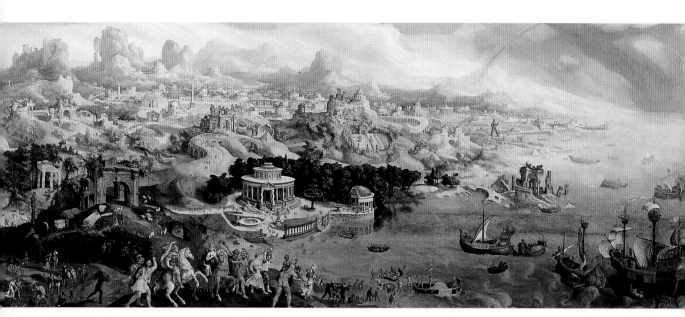

Maerten van Heemskerck
(Dutch, Haarlem, 1498-1574; active in Rome, 1532-36)
Panoramic Fantasy with the Abduction of Helen, 1535
Oil on canvas, 58 x 151 ins (147.3 x 383.5 cm)
Bequest of Henry Walters, 1931; 37.656

Heemskerck painted this homage to ancient art in Rome, where he traveled to study antiquities as well as the work of contemporary masters such as Michelangelo (1475-1564). In the foreground, Helen and the Trojan prince Paris ride to the waiting ships, unwittingly setting off the Trojan War. Throughout the rest of the painting, details of architecture and sculpture from classical antiquity, including such re-creations of the Wonders of the Ancient World as the Colossus of Rhodes and the pyramids, have built up an intriguing picture-puzzle.

Mourner (opposite)
(French, c. 1450)
Alabaster, height 17 ³/₁₆ ins (43.7 cm)
Bequest of Henry Walters, 1931; 27.339

In honoring the dead, funeral monuments of the late Middle Ages often re-created funeral processions through a cloister by placing figures of mourners in an arcade around the sides of the tomb. The tomb carved by the sculptor Claus Sluter (active 1375-1405) for the Burgundian Duke Philip the Bold (1342-1404) in Dijon was the first featuring freestanding figures within a three-dimensional arcade. The Walters mourning monk must come from a slightly later tomb influenced by Sluter's new realism and monumentality.

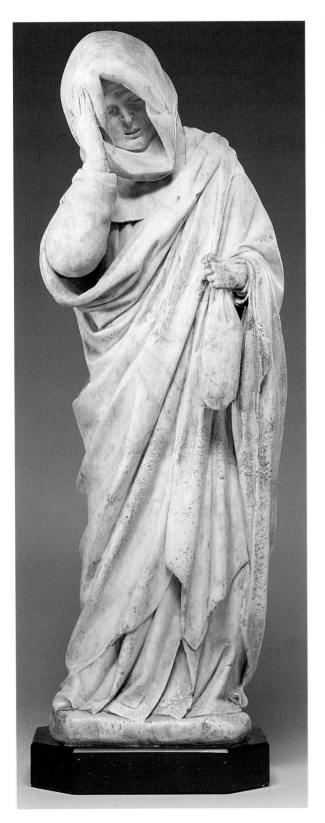

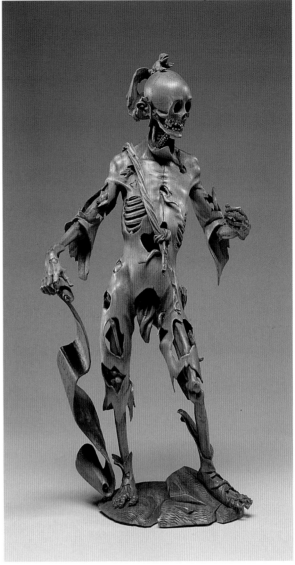

Figure of Death
(German, mid-sixteenth century)
Boxwood, height 9 ¾ ins (24.7 cm)
Bequest of Henry Walters, 1931; 61.97

The scroll held by this figure of death, imagined as
a gruesome cadaver, bears a Latin inscription that
translates: "I am what you will be. I was what you are:
For every man is this so." Death in the form of a walking
cadaver was a common image in northern European
piety during the sixteenth century, and served as a
memento mori, or reminder of human mortality. The
subject was often carved in boxwood, a fine-grain wood
that permits an astonishing degree of undercutting.

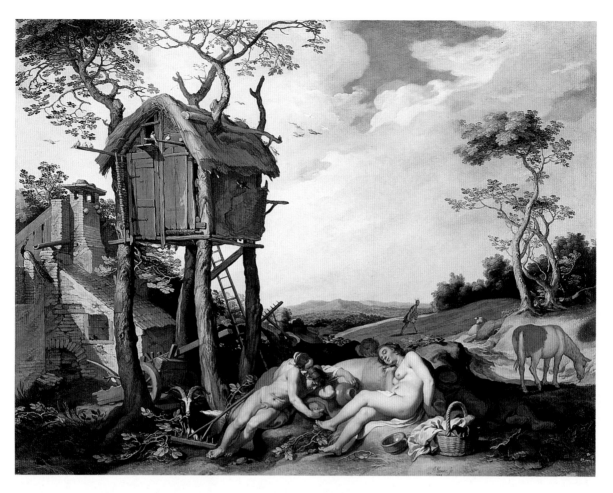

Abraham Bloemart
(Dutch, Utrecht, 1566-1651)
The Parable of the Wheat and the Tares, 1624
Oil on canvas, 39 ½ x 52 ³⁄₁₆ ins (100.4 x 132.5 cm)
Gift of the Dr. Francis D. Murnaghan Fund, 1973; 37.2505

Bloemart combined his skills as a landscapist and a figure painter in this depiction of a parable from the Gospel of Matthew. The sleeping peasants are unaware of the devil sowing tares, or weeds, in the field where they should have sown wheat. The message that laziness is fertile ground for sin is brought out through Bloemart's smooth, sensuous style, especially in the depiction of the two sleepers, whose incongruous nakedness reminded the contemporary viewer that the human tendency to sin goes back to Adam and Eve.

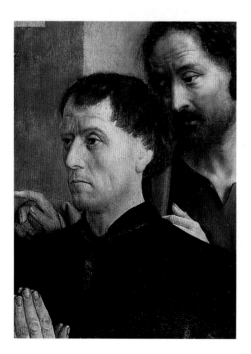

Hugo van der Goes
(Flemish, Ghent, c. 1435-82)
Donor with St. John the Baptist, c. 1475-80
Oil on panel, 12 ¹¹⁄₁₆ x 8 ⅞ ins (32.2 x 22.5 cm)
Bequest of Henry Walters, 1931; 37.296

Hugo van der Goes, famous for the sensitivity of his portrayals, has here created an image of intense spiritual concentration. This small panel depicting an unidentified donor was cut at the top and bottom. It most likely once formed the wing of a diptych, with the other wing representing the Virgin and Child. It is to these figures that the devotion of the praying man is directed.

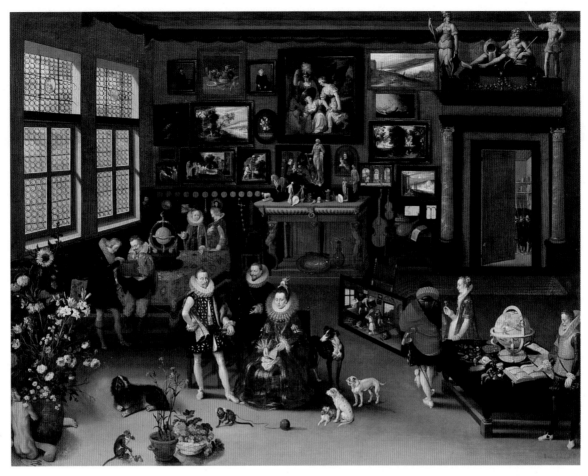

Frans Francken II and workshop, with Jan Brueghel II
(Flemish, Antwerp, 1601-78 and 1581-1642)
The Archdukes Albert and Isabella in a Collector's Cabinet, c. 1626
Oil on panel, 37 x 48 ⁹⁄₁₆ ins (94 x 123.3 cm)
Museum Purchase, 1948; 37.2010

In this depiction of an ideal collector's cabinet or chamber with its encyclopedic variety of curiosities and artworks, the collection is being validated by the visit of the Archdukes Albert (1559-1621) and Isabella (1566-1633), rulers of the Spanish Netherlands and important patrons of the arts. Such cabinets were popular in the seventeenth century and were often the subject of paintings and prints. These representations reflect contemporary interest in expressing the totality of the universe by bringing together natural objects from all over the world (Naturalia) and works of art and scientific instruments (Artificialia).

Cornelis van Poelenburch
(Dutch, Utrecht, 1585-1667)
Portrait of Jan Pellicorne, c. 1626
Oil on copper, 2 ¹⁵⁄₁₆ x 3 ⅞ ins (7.5 x 9.8 cm)
Gift of the A. Jay Fink Foundation, Inc., Baltimore,
in memory of Abraham Jay Fink, 1963; 38.226

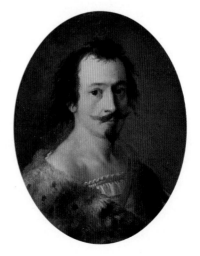

This miniature and its pendant portraying Pellicorne's wife, Susanna van Collen, were probably made to celebrate the couple's marriage in 1626, the year after Poelenburch's return to Utrecht from Italy. The bridegroom, an Amsterdam merchant, is portrayed in the garb of an Arcadian shepherd, wearing a leopard skin, a blouse, and with tousled hair. Romantic views of the supposedly care-free life of shepherds were popular with the social elite in seventeenth-century Netherlands and stemmed from a revival of interest in the writings of the Roman poet Virgil (first century BC).

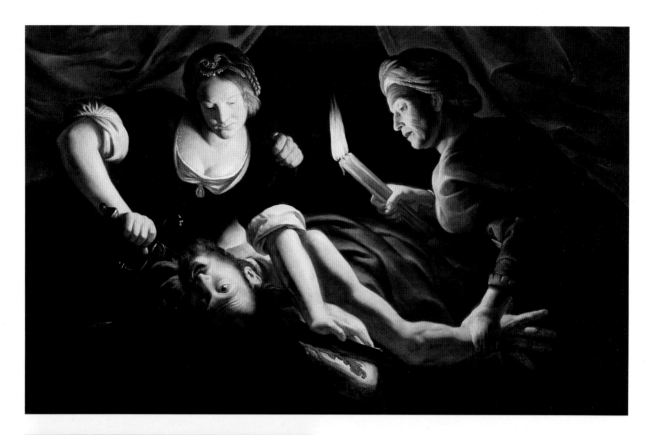

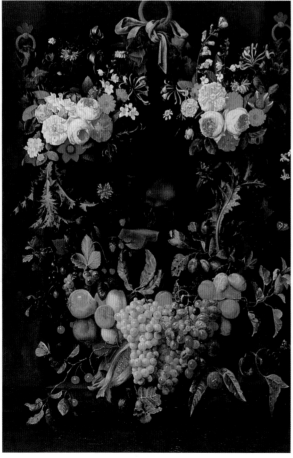

The Candlelight Master
(French, active c. 1630-40)
Judith and Holofernes, c. 1640
Oil on canvas, 49 ½ x 77 ½ ins (125.7 x 196.8 cm)
Bequest of Henry Walters, 1931; 37.653

In this striking depiction of Judith, the Old Testament
heroine who beheaded the Assyrian general Holofernes,
the as-yet unidentified artist nicknamed for his
fascination with candlelight, has heightened the
drama by using a candle as the single powerful
light source and by contrasting the horrifying face
of Holofernes with the determined, serene countenance
of Judith.

Joris van Son
(Flemish, Antwerp, 1613-67)
Floral Still Life with Vanitas, c. 1658-60
Oil on canvas, 49 ⅛ x 36 ½ ins (124.7 x 92.7 cm)
Bequest of Mrs. Marcelle J. von Mayer-Denues, 1985; 37.2623

Joris van Son has painted an elaborate garland to
surround a *vanitas*, a still life composed of objects
reminding the viewer of the brevity of life: a skull,
a candle quickly burning, and an hourglass. Such
masterfully painted assemblages of flowers and fruit
were often used in the seventeenth century to frame
images of spiritual significance. Here the beautiful
garland itself shows signs of decay: nibbled leaves
and thistles around the *vanitas* strike a disturbing
note among the bountiful fruit and flowers.

Eighteenth & Nineteenth Century Art

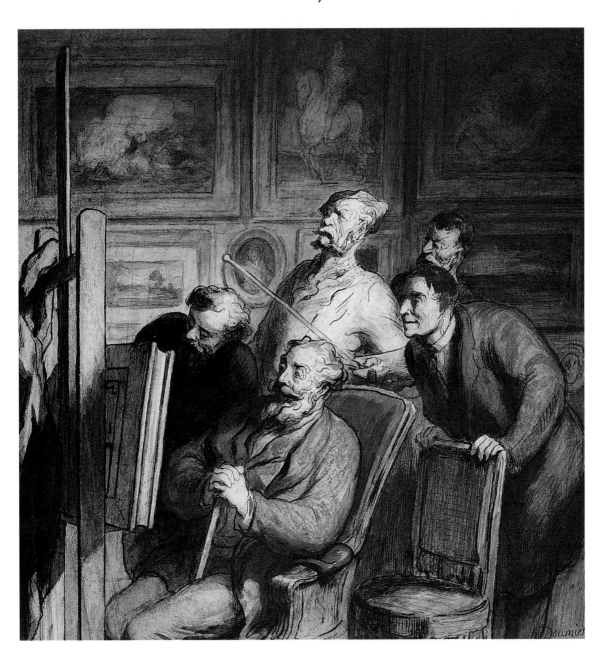

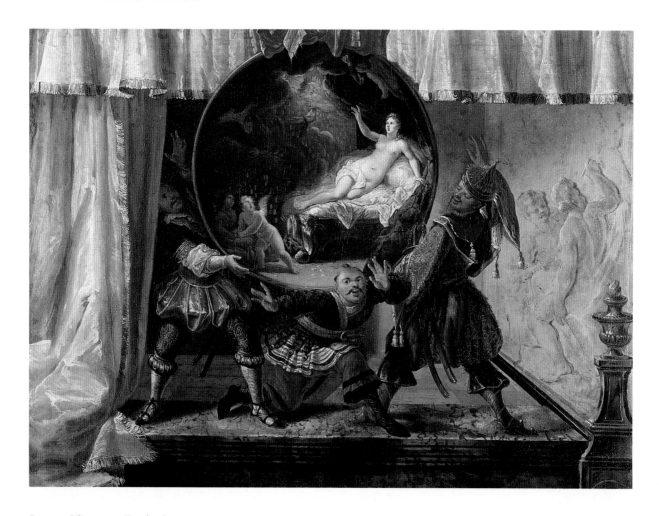

Jacques Vigoureux Duplessis
(French, active 1700-30)
Painted Fire Screen, 1700
Oil on fabric, 34 ¼ x 48 ⅛ ins (87 x 122 cm)
Museum Purchase, 1972; 37.2479

Originally mounted as a screen to cover a fireplace
during warm weather, in this exotic painting the artist
has transformed the hearth into a miniature stage. Three
fanciful Chinese characters hold aloft a circular screen
on which is depicted the mythological story of Zeus
showering Danaë with gold. A pair of figures, painted
in grisaille on the side wall, incise their names on a tree
trunk, a motif symbolizing eternal love. The fire screen
is the earliest recorded work of Vigoureux Duplessis, an
artist who was associated with decorative projects for
the Paris Opera, the Royal Academy of Music, and the
Beauvais Tapestry Manufactory.

Jean-Marc Nattier (opposite)
(French, Paris, 1685-1766)
**Miniature Portrait of César-François Cassini de Thury,
c. 1750**
Watercolor on ivory, 3 ⅛ x 2 ¾ ins (8 x 6.9 cm)
Bequest of Henry Walters, 1931; 38.101

Nattier, who was regarded as one of the foremost
portrait painters at the court of Louis XV (reigned
1715-74), occasionally turned to miniature painting,
as demonstrated by this likeness of Cassini de Thury
(1714-84), a distinguished astronomer and Director of
the Paris Observatory, who is shown at his desk
taking a pinch of snuff from a gold box.

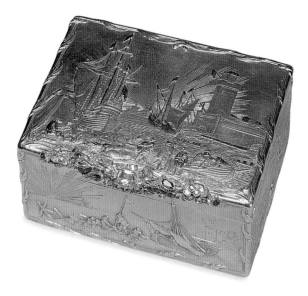

Jean George
(French, Paris, master 1752-died 1765)
Snuffbox, 1758-59
Quatre couleur gold, engraved, diamonds and emeralds,
1 ⅝ x 3 ¼ x 2 ½ ins (4 x 8 x 6.4 cm)
Bequest of Henry Walters, 1931; 57.95

In western Europe during the eighteenth century, small
boxes, ostensibly snuff containers, executed in gold and
other precious materials, were among the most prized,
luxury products. In this example, the master goldsmith
Jean George worked in several colors of gold, the
differences being achieved by using different alloys, a
technique known as *quatre couleur*. The images on the
six surfaces of the box recall the harbor scenes of the
painter Joseph Vernet (1714-89).

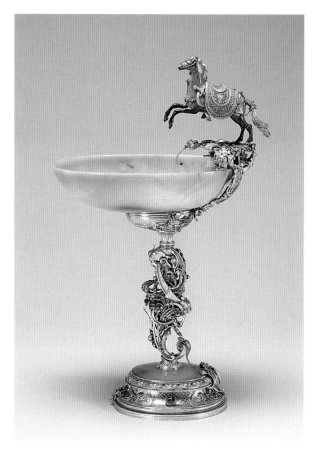

Johann Melchior Dinglinger
(German, Dresden, 1664-1731)
Ceremonial Cup, before 1722
Agate, gold, enamel, silver, parcel gilt, and semi-precious stones,
height 11 ⅜ ins (29 cm)
Museum Purchase, 1971; 57.1994

This magnificent late-Baroque ceremonial cup was made
for Augustus the Strong (1670-1733), Elector of Saxony
and King of Poland. One of a pair, it was first exhibited
in 1722 in the Green Vaults of Dresden, the royal treasury
opened as a public museum the following year. A prancing
Polish horse is mounted on an agate bowl. Protruding from
his elaborately enameled saddle cover are the handles
of the ceremonial sword of Poland and of the sword of
Investiture of the Order of the White Eagle. A rider
and horse enameled on an oval plaque on the back of
the cup represents Lithuania, then united with Poland.
Other insignia include the crown of Poland placed on
a crimson cushion, the Polish white eagle and the
monarch's monogram. Dogs and salamanders are
among the naturalistic elements incorporated into
the exuberant scroll-work of the mount.

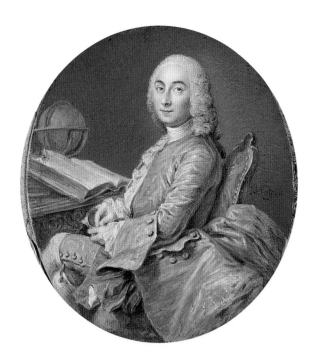

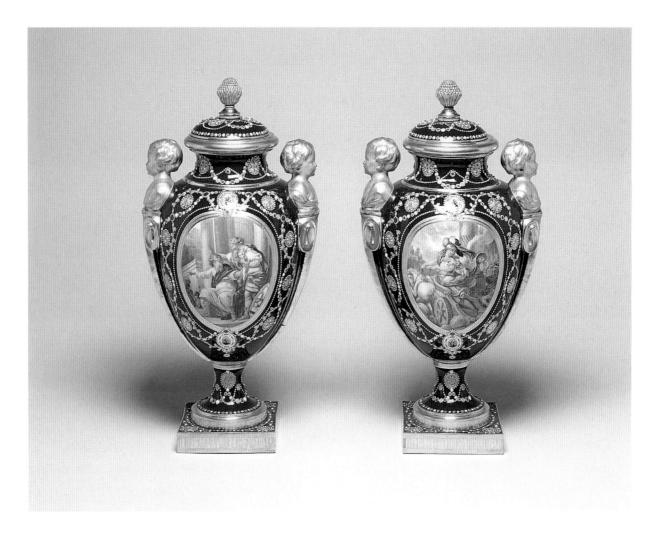

Two Vases *(Vases des âges à têtes d'enfants)*
(French, Sèvres, 1780-81)
Soft-paste porcelain, height 14 ins (35.5 cm)
Bequest of Henry Walters, 1931; 48.566-567

These vases with handles in the form of infants' heads,
together with three others with handles modeled as the
busts of young women and bearded men, now in the
J. Paul Getty Museum, Malibu, constituted a garniture
known as the *Vases des âges*. Among the most lavish
porcelains ever produced at Sèvres, these pieces were
purchased by Louis XVI (1754-93) for the Château of
Versailles in 1781.

Many of the manufactory's foremost talents
participated in the production of these porcelains.
Jacques-François Deparis, with the assistance of
Louis-Simon Boizot, designed the neo-classical
shapes. The miniature scenes in the reserves were
painted by Antoine Caton copying illustrations
from the 1773 edition of François de Salignac de la
Mothe-Fénélon's *Les Aventures de Télémarque*.
Etienne-Henry Le Guay *père* was responsible
for the gilding and the "jewels," actually drops
of translucent enamel over stamped gold foils, were the
work of Philippe Parpette.

Jean-Auguste-Dominique Ingres (opposite)
(French, Montauban, 1780-Paris, 1867)
**The Betrothal of Raphael and the Niece of
Cardinal Bibbiena, 1813**
Oil on paper mounted on fabric, 23 ⅜ x 18 ¼ ins
(59.3 x 46.3 cm)
Bequest of Henry Walters, 1931; 37.13

Ingres, the foremost exponent of the classical tradition
in French art during the nineteenth century, drew
inspiration from ancient Greek and Roman sources
and from the High Renaissance. He intended to produce
a series of works recording incidents in the life of
Raphael (1483-1520), whom he idolized, but only
completed several. In this example, Cardinal Dovizi
il Bibbiena offers his niece in marriage to Raphael. The
image of the cardinal was based on a portrait by Raphael
in the Pitti Palace, Florence, whereas the likeness of the
young artist is drawn from a work by Raphael in the
National Gallery of Art, Washington, DC.

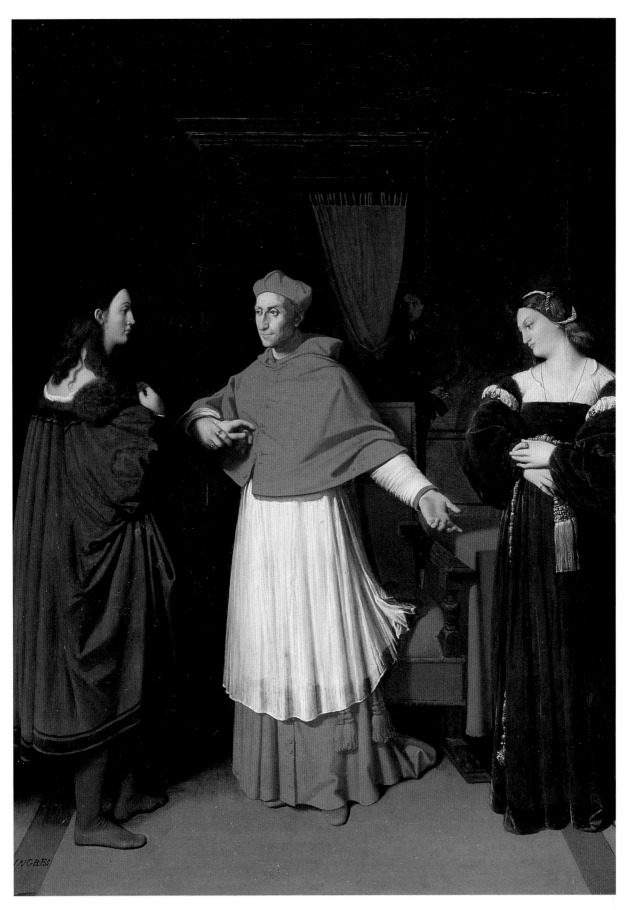

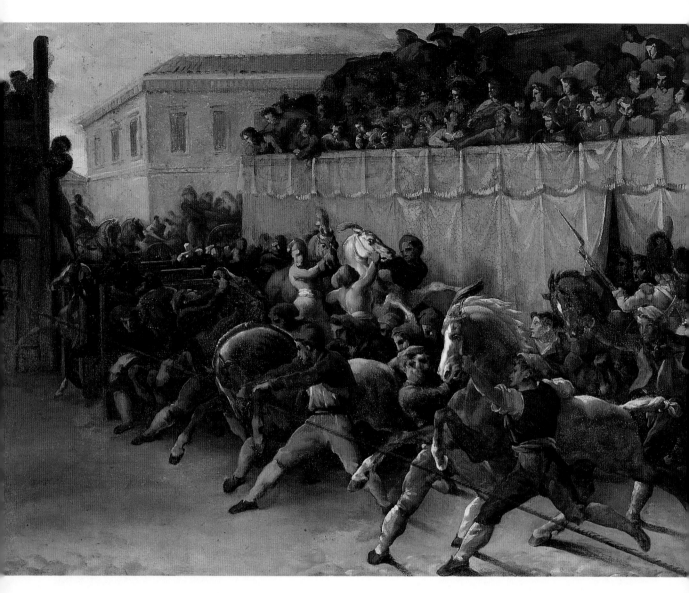

Jean-Louis-André-Théodore Géricault
(French, Rouen, 1791-Paris, 1824)
The Riderless Racers at Rome, 1817
Oil on paper mounted on fabric, 17 ⁹⁄₁₆ x 23 ⅜ ins
(44.5 x 59.5 cm)
Bequest of Henry Walters, 1931; 37.189

As a keen equestrian, Géricault was attracted to subjects
involving horses. While studying in Rome in 1817, he
witnessed the *corsa dei barberi*, the famous race of the
riderless Barbary horses at the close of Carnival. To
prepare for painting a monumental canvas recording the
spectacle, Géricault executed some oil sketches. In this
study, showing the grooms struggling to hold the horses
at the starting line on the Via del Corso, he presents the
most literal rendition of the event, whereas in many of
the other sketches he sets the race in antiquity,
introducing nude figures and classical architecture.

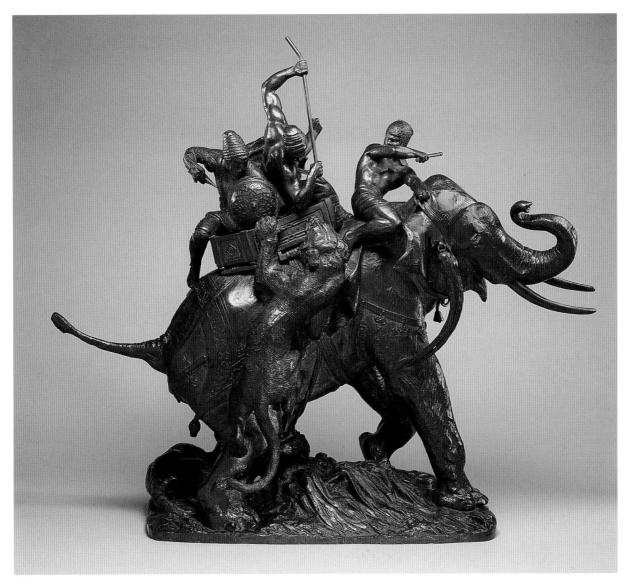

Antoine-Louis Barye
(French, Paris, 1796-1875)
The Tiger Hunt, 1834-37
Bronze, height 27 ¹¹⁄₁₆ ins (69.8 cm)
Bequest of Henry Walters, 1931; 27.176

In 1834 the Duke of Orleans (1810-42) commissioned
a monumental *surtout de table* or table center-piece that
was to be executed after the designs of Aimé Chenavard
by a number of artists including James Pradier and
Jean-Baptiste-Jules Klagmann as well as Barye. The

central element in the project, and the first component
to be completed, was *The Tiger Hunt* which, after being
modeled by Barye, assisted by Auguste Louis Marie
Ottin, was cast by Honoré Gonon.

The completed *surtout de table* was delivered to
Versailles in 1839, but was dispersed following the
duke's untimely death in 1843. Lateral elements in
the composition, including Bayre's *The Lion Hunt*,
The Wild Bull Hunt, *The Bear Hunt* and *The Elk Hunt*,
were eventually reunited in the collection by William
and Henry Walters.

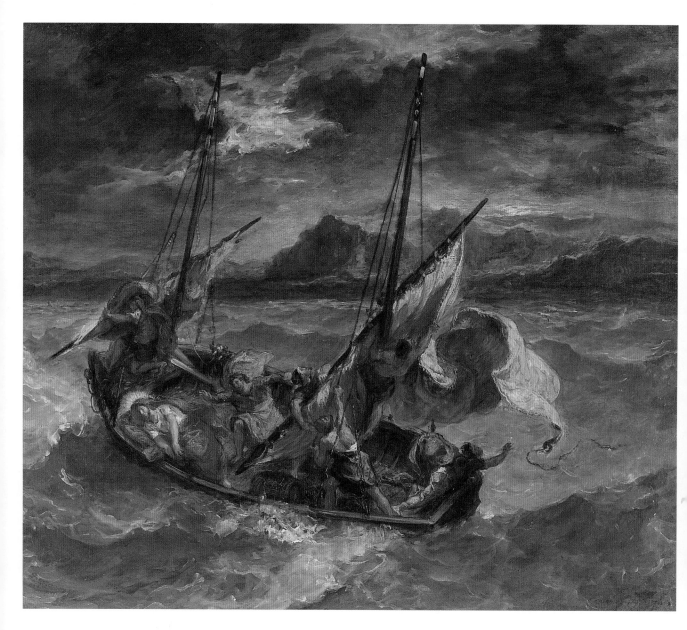

Ferdinand Victor Eugène Delacroix
(French, Charenton-Saint-Maurice, 1897-Paris, 1863)
Christ on the Sea of Galilee, 1854
Oil on fabric, 23 ½ x 28 ⅞ ins (59.8 x 73.3 cm)
Bequest of Henry Walters, 1931; 37.186

This scene, with a storm, raging water, and turbulent sky, is the most dramatic in a series that Delacroix painted dealing with Christ's stilling of the tempest.

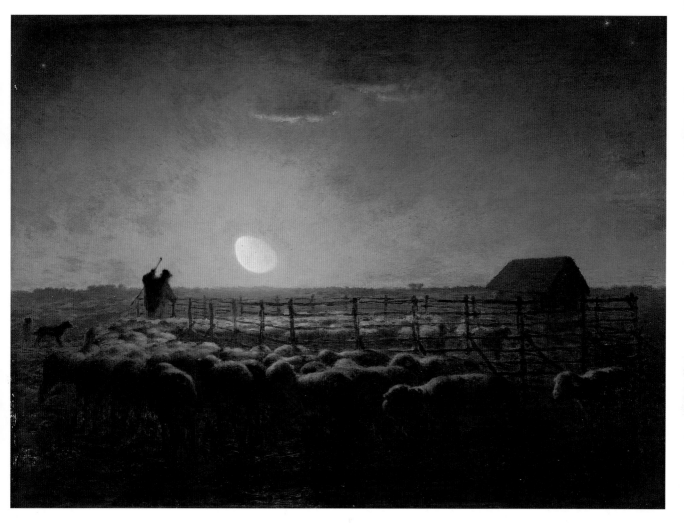

Jean-François Millet
(French, Gruchy, 1814-Barbizon, 1875)
The Sheepfold, Moonlight, 1856-60
Oil on panel, 17 ⅞ x 24 ⅞ ins (43.6 x 63.4 cm)
Bequest of Henry Walters, 1931; 37.30

Of this painting Millet wrote:
  "Oh, I wish I could make those who see my work
  feel the splendors and terrors of the night! One
  ought to be able to make people hear the songs,
  the silences, and the murmurings of the air."

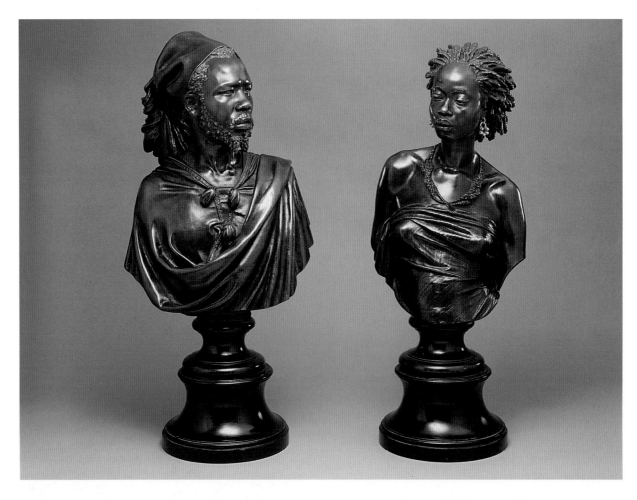

Saïd Abdullah of the Mayac, Kingdom of Darfur (Sudan), 1848
African Venus, 1851
Bronze, height 16 ½ ins (42 cm) and 15 ½ ins (39 cm)
Museum Purchase, 1991; 54.2664 and 54.2665

Cordier submitted a plaster cast of the bust of an African visitor to Paris to the Salon of 1848, and two years later he again entered it as a bronze. A young African woman served as the model for the companion piece in 1851. Regarded as powerful expressions of nobility and dignity, these sculptures proved to be highly popular: casts were acquired by the Museum of National History in Paris and also by Queen Victoria. The Walters pair were cast by the Paris foundry Eck and Durand in 1852.

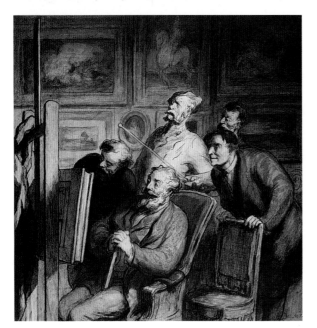

Honoré-Victorin Daumier
(French, Marseilles, 1808-Valmondois, 1879)
The Amateurs, after 1862
Crayon, watercolor, ink and gouache, 12 ¾ x 12 ³⁄₁₆ ins
(32.4 x 31 cm)
Bequest of Henry Walters, 1931; 37.1228

In the 1860s the great caricaturist Daumier produced a number of drawings exploring the reactions of viewers to works of art. In this example, one of several set in a studio, the haughty, aloof artist awaits the presumably enthusiastic responses of his visitors.

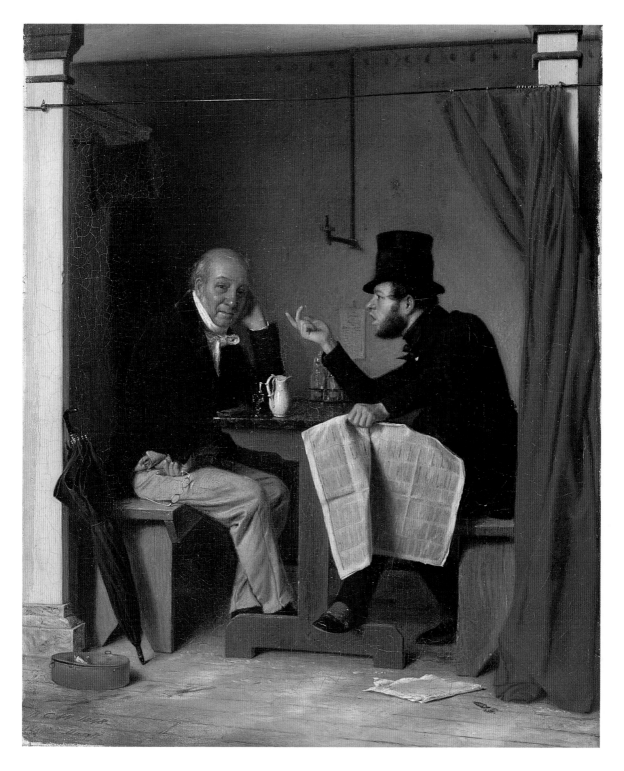

Richard Caton Woodville
(American, Baltimore, 1825-London, 1855)
Politics in an Oyster House, 1848
Oil on fabric, 16 x 13 ins (40.6 x 33 cm)
Gift of C. Morgan Marshall, 1945; 37.1994

During a brief career Woodville produced a number of paintings which serve as key documents of urban life in pre-Civil War America. After training in his native

Baltimore, Woodville traveled to Düsseldorf to enroll in the town's renowned art academy. He remained in Germany for six years and then briefly visited Paris and London before his early death at the age of thirty. While an expatriate, Woodville painted small, anecdotal genre scenes recalling life in Baltimore. The humor he usually imparted to his subjects is illustrated in this typical Baltimore scene showing local individuals, seated in the booth of an oyster house, engaged in conversation.

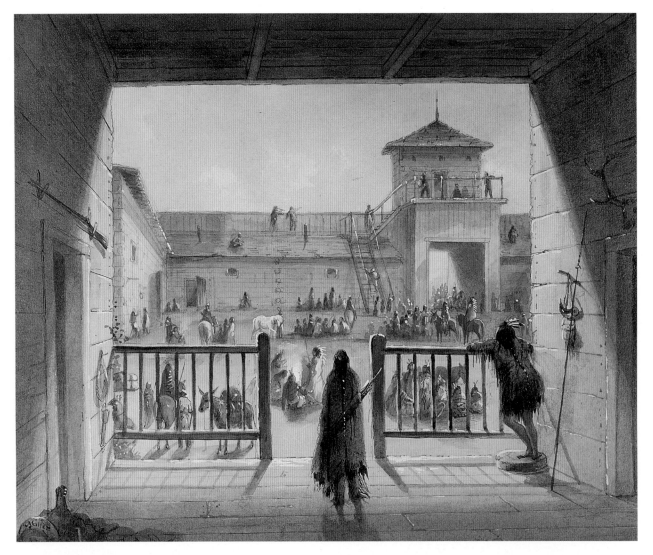

Alfred Jacob Miller
(American, Baltimore, 1810-74)
Interior of Fort Laramie, 1858-60
Watercolor on paper, 11 ⅝ x 14 ⅛ ins (29.5 x 36 cm)
Bequest of Henry Walters, 1931; 37.1940.150

In the spring of 1837, Miller accompanied the Scottish adventurer Captain William Drummond Stewart (died 1871) to the fur traders' rendezvous held that year on the Green River in western Wyoming. At these gatherings trappers and Indians sold their furs and replenished supplies for the following winter. Miller subsequently used the sketches drawn on the trail as the basis for oil paintings for Stewart's ancestral estate, Murthly Castle in Perthshire, Scotland. After returning to Baltimore in 1842, he continued to replicate his sketches in oils and watercolors for American clients. In this scene Miller has provided the only visual record of the first Fort Laramie erected in 1834. Located in eastern Wyoming, the Fort marked the beginning of what would later become the Oregon Trail, the route that was taken by settlers moving West.

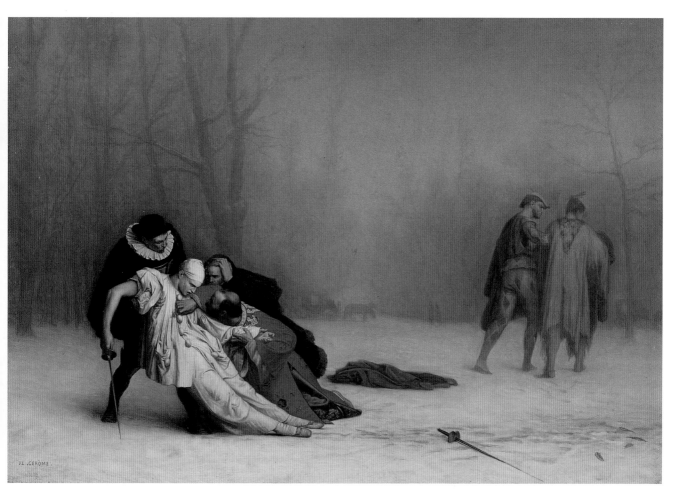

Jean-Léon Gérôme
(French, Vesoul, 1824-Paris, 1904)
The Duel after the Masquerade, 1857-59
Oil on fabric, 15 ⅜ x 22 ⅛ ins (39.1 x 56.3 cm)
Bequest of Henry Walters, 1931; 37.51

In this painting, showing the outcome of a duel after a costume ball, Gérôme replicates, with slight variations, a composition he had executed for the Duc d'Aumale in 1857. It is dawn on a wintry day in the Bois de Boulogne, Paris, and Pierrot succumbs in the arms of the Duc de Guise. A Venetian doge examines Pierrot's wound while Domino clasps his head in despair. To the right, the victorious American Indian departs, accompanied by Harlequin.

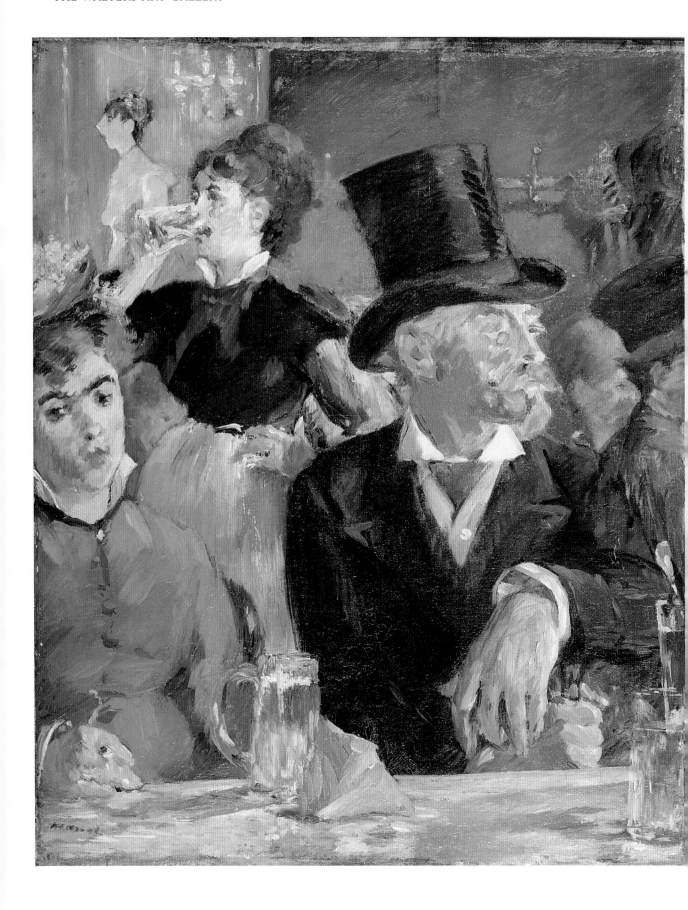

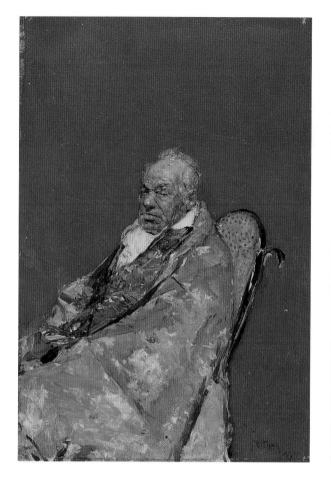

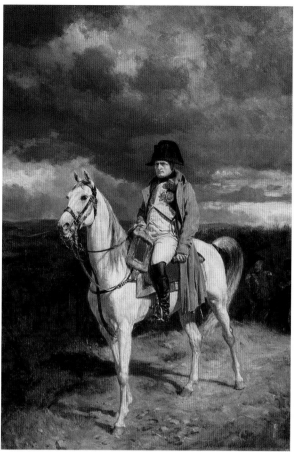

Mariano José-Maria-Bernardo Fortuny y Marsal
(Catalan, Reus, 1838-Rome, 1874)
An Ecclesiastic, c. 1874
Oil on panel, 7 ½ x 5 ⅛ ins (19 x 13 cm)
Bequest of Henry Walters, 1931; 37.150

The Catalan painter Fortuny led a cosmopolitan
existence working closely with colleagues in Spain,
France, and Italy. Not only was he a brilliant technician,
but he proved to be remarkably receptive to progressive
trends. This expressive image of an ecclesiastic in rose-
colored robes posed against a vermilion background,
demonstrates the painter's audacious use of color.

Jean-Louis-Ernest Meissonier
(French, Lyons, 1815-Paris, 1891)
1814, painted 1862
Oil on panel, 12 ¾ x 9 ½ ins (32.4 x 24.2 cm)
Bequest of Henry Walters, 1931; 37.52

After accompanying the French army in the Austro-
Italian War of 1859, Meissonier abandoned the small,
Dutch seventeenth-century genre subjects for which
he had become known and turned with even greater
success to depicting events in the career of Napoleon I.
In this small painting commissioned by the subject's
nephew, Prince Napoleon, the Emperor is portrayed
in a forbidding landscape just after his last, hard-won
victory in the 1814 French campaign which was fought
at Arcis-sur-Aube, near Troyes: 23,000 French troops
withstood the onslaught of 90,000 Austrians, but were
unable to capitalize on their victory.

Edouard Manet (opposite)
(French, Paris, 1832-83)
At the Café, 1879
Oil on canvas, 18 ⅝ x 15 ⅜ ins (47.3 x 39.1 cm)
Bequest of Henry Walters, 1931; 37.893

Toward the end of his career, Manet, a pioneering realist,
undertook several paintings depicting scenes in the

interior of the Brasserie de Reichshoffen in Paris. The
most developed of these, *At the Café*, shows an older
gentleman and a young woman seated at the counter
of the crowded café. An image of the singer is reflected
in the mirror on the back wall. Because of these figures'
dispassionate expressions and their self-absorption,
At the Café has been interpreted as an indictment of the
isolation of the individual in modern society.

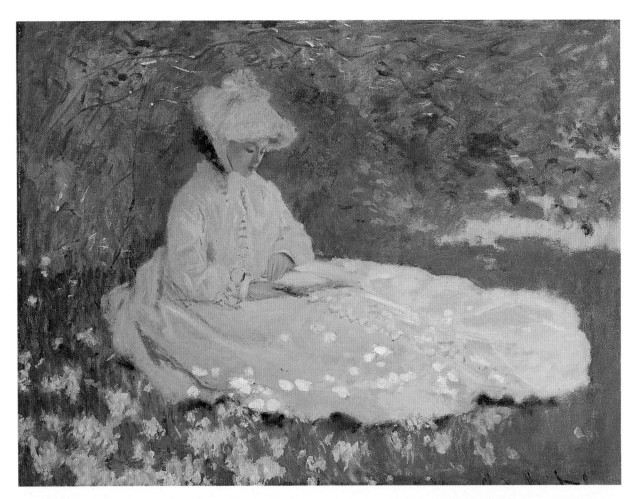

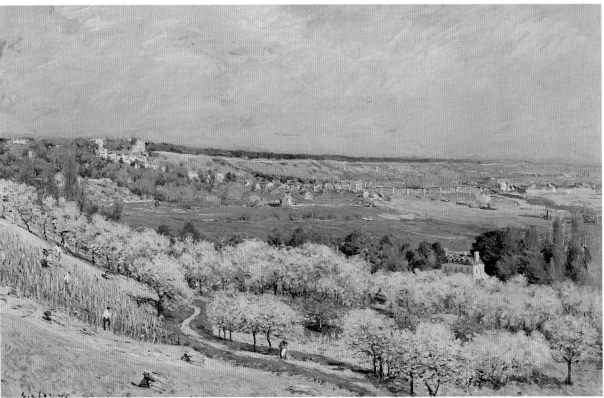

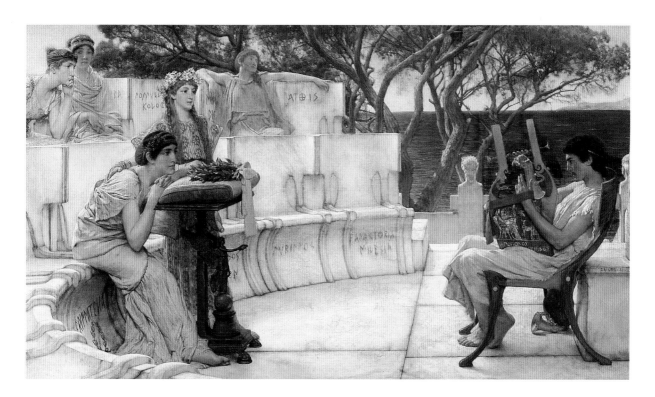

Sir Lawrence Alma-Tadema, RA, OM
(Dutch, Dronrijp, 1836-Wiesbaden, 1912)
Sappho and Alcaeus (Opus CCXXIII), 1881
Oil on panel, 26 x 48 ins (66 x 121.9 cm)
Bequest of Henry Walters, 1931; 37.159

In 1870, the Dutch-born, Belgian-trained artist
Alma-Tadema moved to London where he found
a ready market among the wealthy middle classes
for paintings re-creating scenes of domestic life in
imperial Roman times.

In this work, however, he turns to early Greece to
illustrate a passage by the poet Hermesianaz (preserved
in Atheneaus, *Deipnosophistae*, "Banquet of the Learned,"
book 2, line 598). On the island of Lesbos (Mytilene), in
the late seventh century BC, Sappho and her companions
listen rapturously as the poet Alcaeus plays a kithara.
Striving for verisimilitude, Alma-Tadema copied the
marble seating of the Theater of Dionysos in Athens,
although he substituted the names of members of
Sappho's sorority for those of the officials incised
on the Athenian prototype.

Oscar-Claude Monet (opposite top)
(French, Paris, 1840-Giverny, 1826)
Springtime, c. 1872
Oil on fabric, 19 ⅝ x 25 ¾ ins (50 x 65.5 cm)
Bequest of Henry Walters, 1931; 37.11

In the 1870s Argenteuil, on the Seine River northwest
of Paris, served as a gathering point for a number of
Impressionist artists. In this fully developed
Impressionist work, Monet portrays his first wife,
Camille, seated on the lawn beneath lilac bushes
in the garden of the Maison Aubry, their first residence
in the Paris suburb.

Alfred Sisley (opposite bottom)
(French, Paris, 1839-Moret, 1899)
The Terrace at Saint-Germain: Spring, 1875
Oil on fabric, 29 x 39 ¼ ins (73.6 x 99.6 cm)
Bequest of Henry Walters, 1931; 37.992

In this unusually expansive view, Sisley portrays the
Seine Valley on a sunny spring day. In the foreground
fruit trees blossom and farmers tend vineyards. On the
heights in the distance is the château in which Louis
XIV's court was originally centered, and the celebrated
terraces overlooking the valley. Elements of modern life
include the iron river bridge and a tugboat pulling barges.

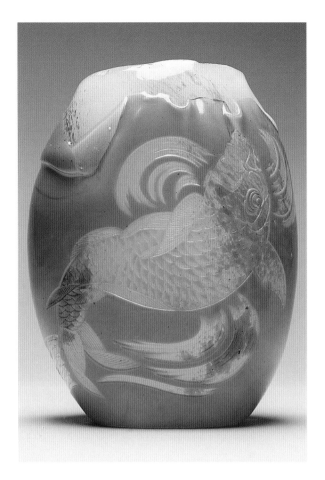

François-Eugène Rousseau
(French, Clichy, 1827-91)
Vase, c. 1878
Glass, encased and engraved, height 7 ins (17.8 cm)
Bequest of Henry Walters, 1931; 47.384

Rousseau was among the first French artists to adapt Japanese motifs to European design. Initially, he specialized in ceramics, but in the late 1870s and early 1880s, Rousseau produced designs for glass manufactured by Appert Frères in Clichy. In this instance, the image of the carp in the swirling waters was taken from an *ukiyo-e* print in Hokusai's *Manga*.

Carl Fabergé
(French, 1846-1920)
Mikhail Perkhin
(Russian, St. Petersburg, active 1884-1903)
Gatchina Palace Egg, 1901
Gold, enamel, seed pearls, height 5 ins (12.5 cm)
Bequest of Henry Walters, 1931; 44.500

Continuing a practice initiated by his father, Alexander III, Czar Nicholas II (1868-1918) presented this egg to his mother, Maria Feodorovna, on Easter Day in 1901. Fabergé's revival of eighteenth-century techniques, including the application of multiple layers of translucent enamel over guilloché or mechanically engraved gold, is demonstrated in the shell of the egg. When opened, the egg reveals a miniature replica of the Gatchina Palace, the Dowager Empress's principal residence outside St. Petersburg. So meticulously did Fabergé's workmaster, Mikhail Perkhin, execute the palace that one can discern such details as cannons, a flag, a statue of Paul I (1754-1801), and elements of the landscape, including parterres and trees.

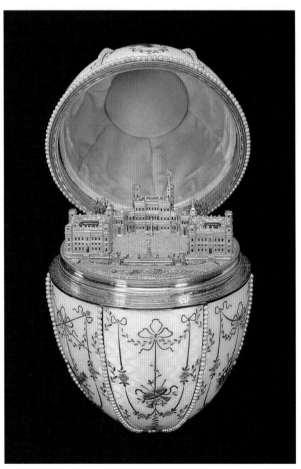

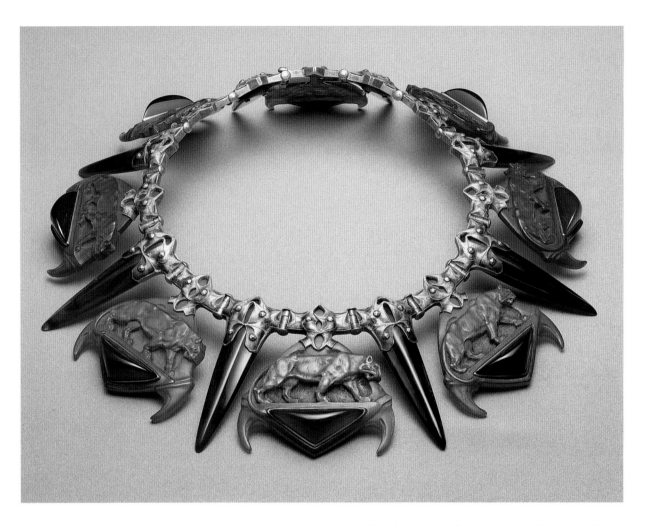

René Lalique
(French, Paris, 1860-1945)
Tiger Necklace, c. 1904
Gold, enamel, horn, tortoise-shell, agate,
diameter 4 ½ ins (10.5cm)
Bequest of Henry Walters, 1931; 57.938

René Lalique revolutionized jewelry design by combining together precious and non-precious materials selected according to their aesthetic appeal. By 1904, the year that he exhibited this necklace at the Louisiana Purchase Exhibition in St. Louis, Lalique had progressed beyond Art Nouveau, the movement with which he was originally associated, and was emphasizing compositions with symmetrical components and the use of animal motifs in a style which would become fully manifested in the designs he created for molded glass several years later.

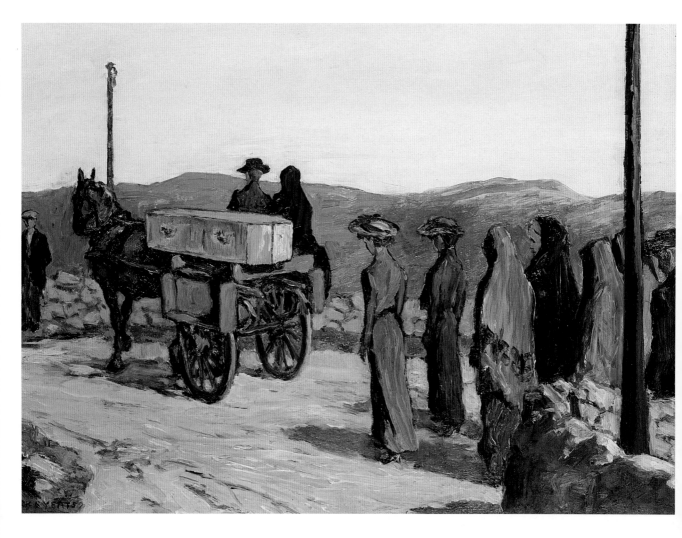

Jack Butler Yeats, RHA
(Irish, London, 1871-Dublin, 1957)
The Swinford Funeral, 1918
Oil on fabric, 9 ⅛ x 14 ¼ ins (23.2 x 36.1 cm)
Gift of the Honorable Francis D. Murnaghan, Jr.; 37.2630

Jack B. Yeats, son of the portraitist, John B. Yeats (1839-1922), and brother of the poet William B. Yeats (1865-1939), is generally acknowledged as the greatest

Irish painter of the first half of the twentieth century. Initially an illustrator, he accompanied the writer, John Millington Synge (1871-1909), on a walking tour of County Mayo in western Ireland in 1905. A sketch made at that time served thirteen years later as the basis for this painting. In referring to the scene in an article he wrote for the *Manchester Guardian*, Synge alluded to several young women in the funeral procession who seemed by their dress to be "returned Americans."

Asian Art

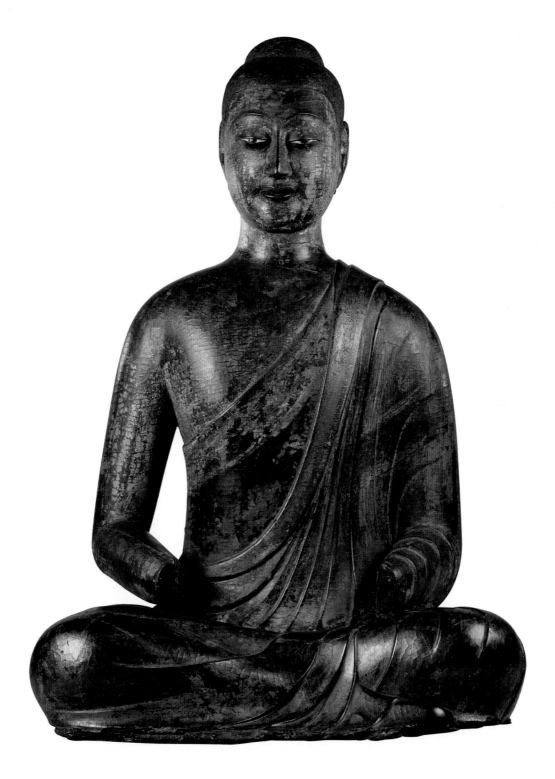

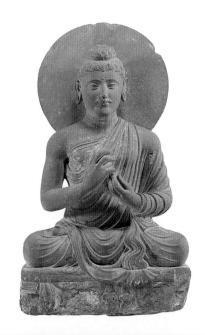

Seated Buddha, in the Attitude of Preaching
(Pakistan, Gandhara, second-third century)
Phyllite, height 24 ¹³/₁₆ ins (63 cm)
Bequest of A. B. Griswold, 1992; 25.123

The Buddha's gesture is associated with his teaching of the fundamental Buddhist truths—how life is inherently unsatisfactory, and how the Buddhist way provides a path of escape.

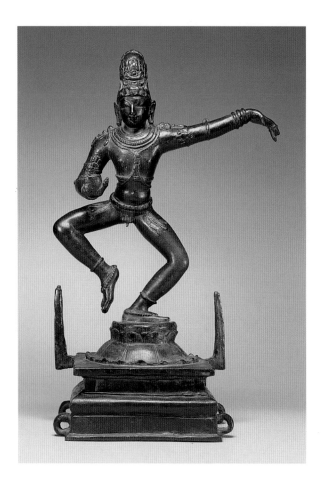

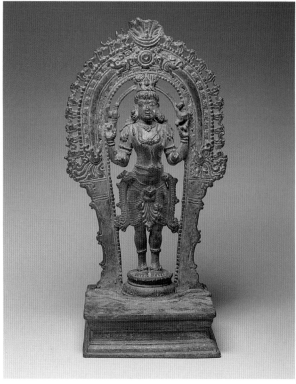

Krishna
(India, Tamil Nadu, Chola dynasty, late tenth century)
Bronze, height 14 ⅛ ins (35.9 cm)
Museum Purchase through the W. Alton Jones Foundation Acquisition Fund, 1993; 54.2850

The youthful Krishna—an incarnation of the supreme Hindu god Vishnu—is shown dancing, as he did after being attacked by the serpent Kaliya, whom he subdued without a struggle. This image was made to be carried in processions on festival days in southern India.

Shiva
(Southern India, Mysore or Kerala, fourteenth-fifteenth century)
Bronze, height 12 ⁵/₁₆ ins (31.3 cm)
Gift of Mr. and Mrs. John Gilmore Ford, 1988; 54.2648

The Hindu god Shiva is shown with expansive chest and alert face, his hands bearing tokens of his exploits—a battle ax, a deer, and (now broken off) a cup of deadly poison. The poison was produced by the gods and demons as they churned up the ocean; when Shiva drank it, it turned his throat blue.

Standing Buddha
(Thailand, Dvaravati period, eighth century)
Sandstone, height 42 ¹⁵⁄₁₆ ins (109 cm)
Bequest of A. B. Griswold, 1992; 25.164

When the Buddhists of ancient Thailand adopted the standing stone Buddha of India as a primary iconic type, the pose was altered (in Thailand, both hands—here broken—perform a teaching gesture), and the canons of Indian beauty lost their firm hold in a drive to achieve an expression of serenity.

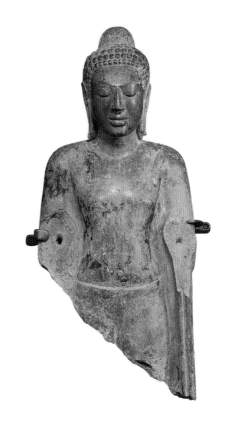

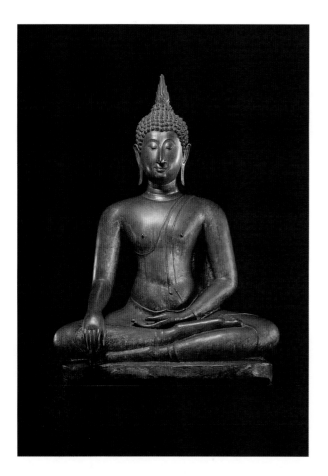

Buddha at the Moment of Victory
(North-central Thailand, second half of the fifteenth century)
Leaded bronze, height 35 ⁷⁄₁₆ ins (92 cm)
Bequest of A. B. Griswold, 1992; 54.2775

The Buddha is depicted at the moment of his victory over the forces of evil, when he took his right hand from his lap (where it had been resting as he meditated) and touched the earth. Following the emergence of Sukhothai as an independent kingdom in the late thirteenth century, a new style of Buddha image was developed in Siam (Thailand). Technical analyses suggest that this image is a later production of one of the Sukhothai workshops.

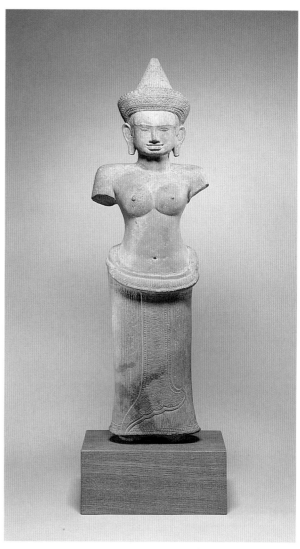

Female Diety
(Cambodia, Angkor Wat period, 1110 - 60)
Sandstone, height 25 ½ ins (64.8 cm)
Gift of Lispenard and Marshall Green, 1994; 25.212

The youthful goddess, wearing a decorated wrap-around skirt that reflects contemporary fashion, may be the spouse of either of the chief Hindu gods, Vishnu or Shiva.

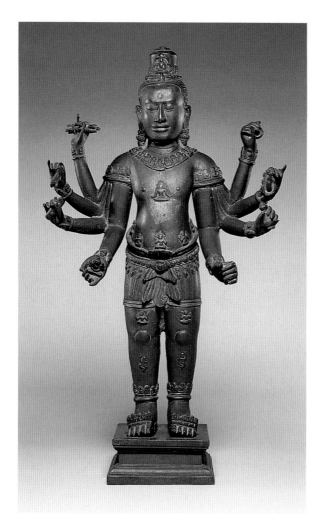

Eight-armed Avalokiteshvara
(Cambodia, Bayon period, late twelfth-early thirteenth century)
Bronze, height 18 ⅞ ins (47.2 cm)
Bequest of A. B. Griswold, 1992; 54.2726

This figure of the Bodhisattva of Compassion is a bronze replica of one of the twenty-three stone images King Jayavarman VII sent to different parts of the kingdom in 1191, in a celebration of the compassion the king attributed to his own father. The small figures of the Buddha can be understood as representing the qualities of Buddhahood that lie in every pore of Avalokiteshvara's skin, and the figures around the waist are an outward manifestation of advanced techniques of meditation.

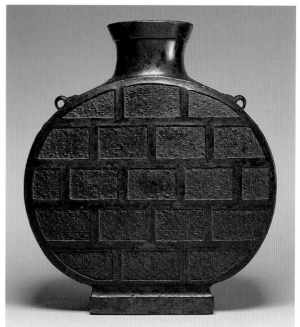

Canteen (pien-hu)
(China, Eastern Chou period, fifth-fourth century BC)
Bronze, height 13 %6 ins (34.5 cm)
Bequest of Henry Walters, 1931; 54.1242

This vessel, made for ceremonial use and then
subsequently deposited in a tomb, dates from a
period in which a major element of interest is
the endless inventiveness of the patterns, which
are here contained within small rectangles.

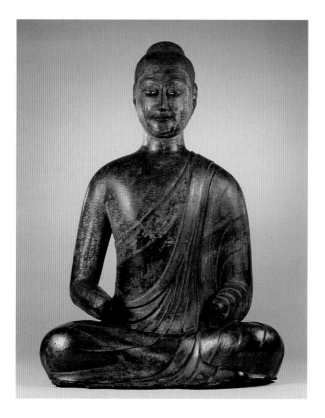

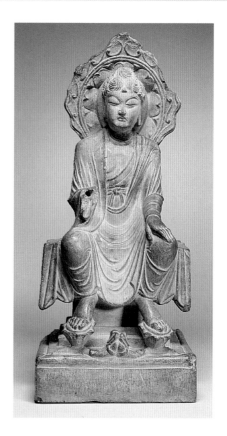

Buddha
(China, Sui dynasty, 690s)
Painted lacquer over wood, height 41 ½ ins (105.4 cm)
Bequest of Henry Walters, 1931; 25.9

Carved from twelve joined pieces of wood, covered with
five layers of lacquer, and then painted, this sculpture is
the oldest Chinese image of the Buddha made with such
a technique known to have survived. It probably depicts
Amitābha, the cosmic Buddha who presides over the
Western Paradise—a place where Buddhists of the
period hoped to be reborn.

Seated Maitreya
(China, T'ang dynasty, first quarter of the eighth century)
Stone, height 17 ⅝ ins (44.7 cm)
Bequest of Henry Walters, 1931; 25.6

The Buddha of the future, who is shown seated upon
a throne, his legs pendant, resides in a heavenly realm
where one can be reborn.

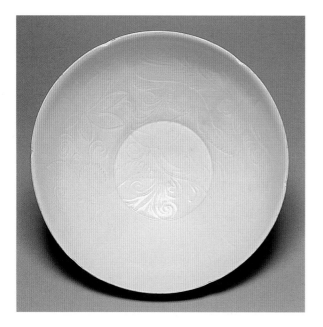

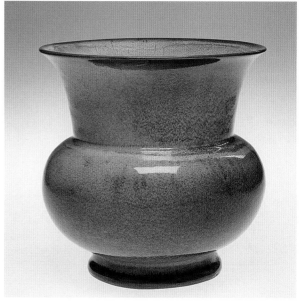

Bowl
(China (Ting-ware kilns), Hopei province, Northern Sung dynasty,
eleventh-twelfth century)
High-fired stoneware with white glaze,
diameter 9 ⅛ ins (23 cm)
Bequest of Henry Walters, 1931; 49.1718

A lotus spray fills the inside walls of the bowl in seeming
organic harmony with its shape.

Flower Pot
(China, Honan province, twelfth-early fifteenth century)
Stoneware with Chün-ware glaze,
height 10 ins (25.4 cm)
Bequest of Henry Walters, 1931; 49.1585

Wares of this sort were made for use by the last
Northern Sung emperor (who reigned from 1101
until 1125), but some authorities believe that this
flower pot and others like it (in the National Palace
Museum, Taipei) date from a later period.

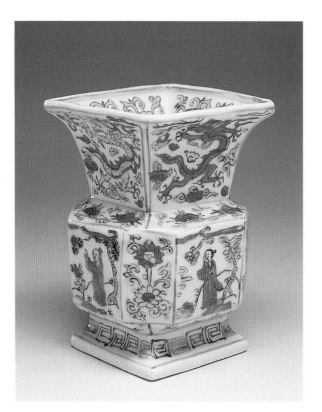

Faceted Vase
(China, Ching-te-chen, Kiangsi province, Ming dynasty,
late sixteenth-early seventeenth century)
Porcelain decorated with underglaze blue and overglaze
enamels, height 4 ⅞ ins (12.4 cm)
Bequest of Henry Walters, 1931; 49.737

This small vase, in the general shape of an ancient
bronze vessel, bears panels depicting a sage alone in the
landscape—a theme of which one could never tire.

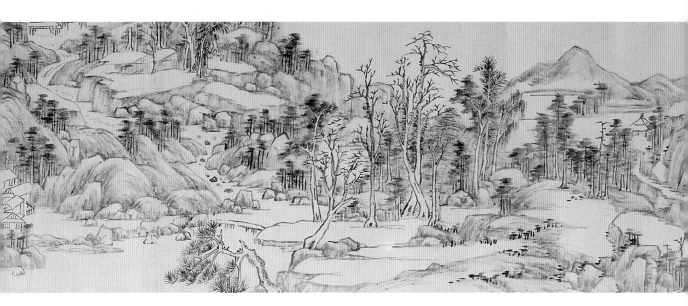

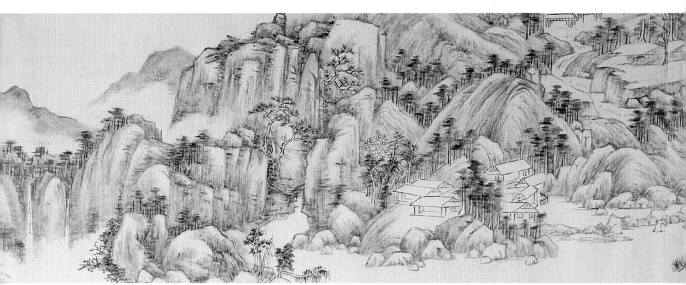

Free Spirits among Streams and Mountains, 1684
(Wang Yüan-ch'i (China), Ch'ing dynasty, 1642-1715)
Handscroll, ink on paper, height 13 ¾ x overall length
279 ⅞ ins (34.93 x 710.9 cm)
Museum Purchase through the W. Alton Jones Foundation
Acquisition Fund, 1994; 35.198

When he painted this long handscroll in 1684, Wang
Yüan-ch'i, the greatest orthodox master of the Ch'ing
dynasty, had not yet developed the style for which he
is best remembered. Grounded in the lessons of his
grandfather, the artist Wang Shih-min, he aimed in his
own way to make a work both as weighty and as free
as that which was regarded as the greatest of Chinese
handscrolls—Huang Kung-wang's *Dwelling in the
Fu-ch'un Mountains* of 1350.

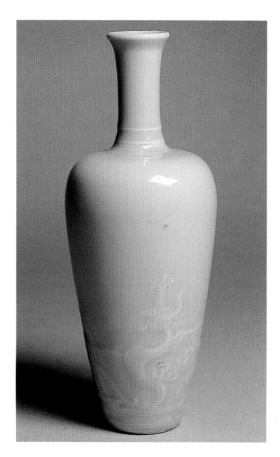

Vase
(China, Ch'ing dynasty, K'ang-hsi period, c. 1710-22)
Porcelain with celadon glaze, height 7 ¹¹/₁₆ ins
(20.6 cm)
Bequest of Henry Walters, 1931; 49.1342

Low-relief dragons rise from the sea on the lower part of this vase, which was made for use in the imperial palace. Vases of this shape—also made with the glaze known as "peach bloom"—belonged on a writing table.

Dish with Flowering Prunus
(China, Ch'ing dynasty, Yung-ch'eng period, 1723-35)
Porcelain with overglaze enamels, Yung-ch'eng mark
(on underside) in underglaze blue, diameter 19 ¾ ins
(50.2 cm)
Bequest of Henry Walters, 1931; 49.2365

This magnificent dish belongs to a set made for use in the palace.

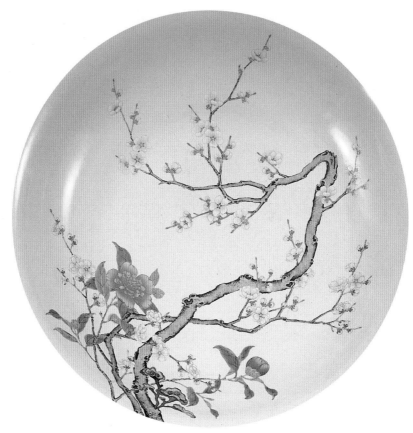

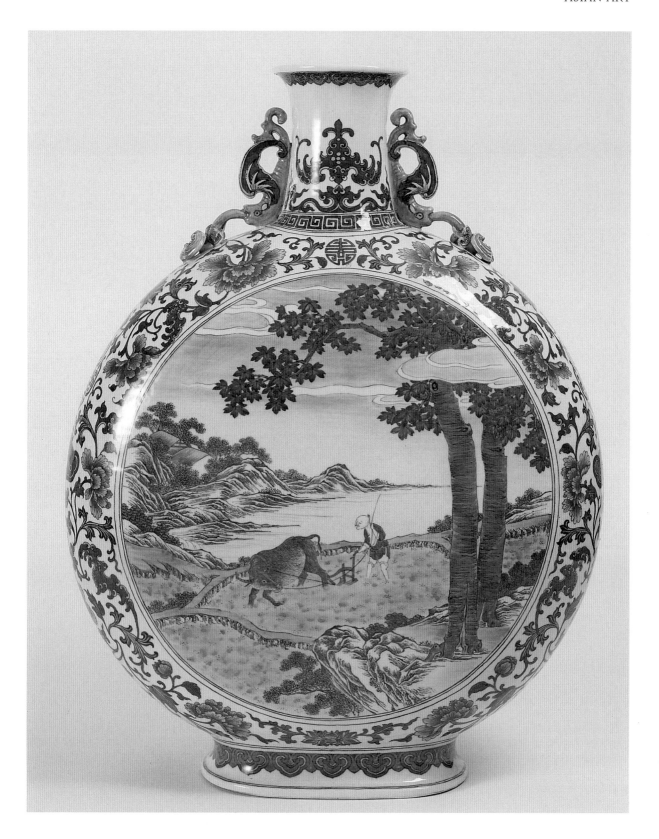

Flask
(China, Ch'ing dynasty, Ch'ien-lung period, 1736-95)
Porcelain decorated in underglaze blue, height 23 ¼ ins (59 cm)
Bequest of Henry Walters, 1931; 49.2015

The outer decoration of this oversize vessel is in the
style of the early Ming dynasty; the scene is adopted
from an illustration in a book showing scenes of
ploughing and weaving, published in 1739.

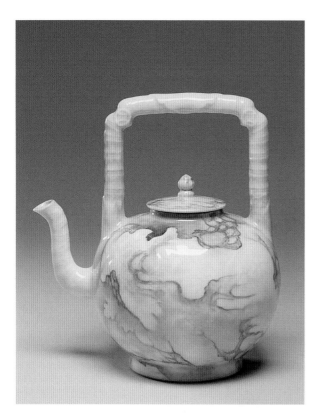

Teapot
(China, Ch'ing dynasty, Ch'ien-lung period, 1736-95, c. 1770s)
Porcelain with overglaze enamel, height 5 ¹¹⁄₁₆ ins
(14.4 cm)
Bequest of Henry Walters, 1931; 49.1938

The body of the vessel was made in a mold that formed chrysanthemums in low relief; then it was decorated with a marbelized pattern within which there is actually a landscape, with mountains, trees, and mist.

Buddha
(Korea, Choson dynasty, c. sixteenth century)
Wood with gilding, height 17 ins (43.2 cm)
Bequest of Henry Walters, 1931; 61.277

With the asymmetrically arranged ends of his robe falling beneath his lotus throne, and floral scrolls and leaping flames enframing him, the Buddha casts a downward glance.

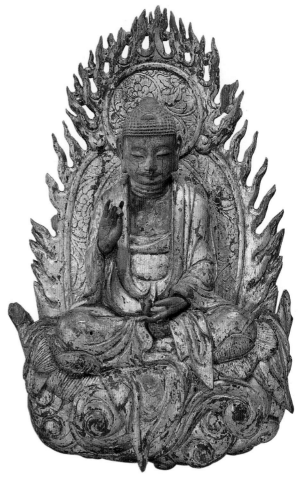

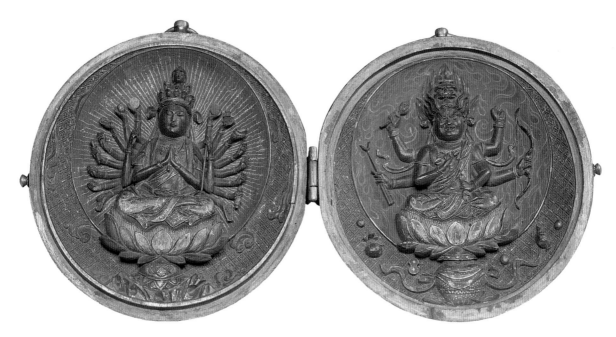

Locket with the Buddhist Deities Juichimen Kannon and Aizen
(Japan, Kamakura period, thirteenth century)
Wood, lacquer, and gilt bronze 2 ⁵⁄₁₆ ins (5.8 cm)
Bequest of Henry Walters, 1931; 61.278

This locket, made to be carried by a Buddhist priest, has likely survived because it was deposited inside a full-size "King of Desire", above whose forehead is featured a lion's head, which stands for the capacity to transform lust into pure love. On the left is a "1,000-armed Kannon" (Sahasrabhujāryāvalokiteśvara), symbolizing compassion for all living creatures.

Naoshige
(Shoraku, Japan, Edo period, died 1780)
Sword Guard
Iron and gold, diameter 2 ¹¹⁄₁₆ ins (6.8 cm)
Bequest of Henry Walters, 1931; 51.236

Selected from among the hundreds of *tsuba* (sword guards) at The Walters is this eighteenth-century example, in which clouds and a dragon (clutching a sacred pearl) seem to float in space.

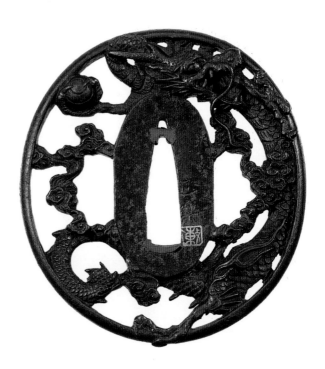

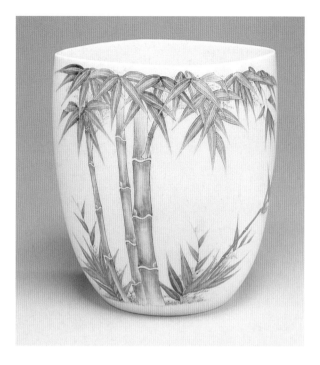

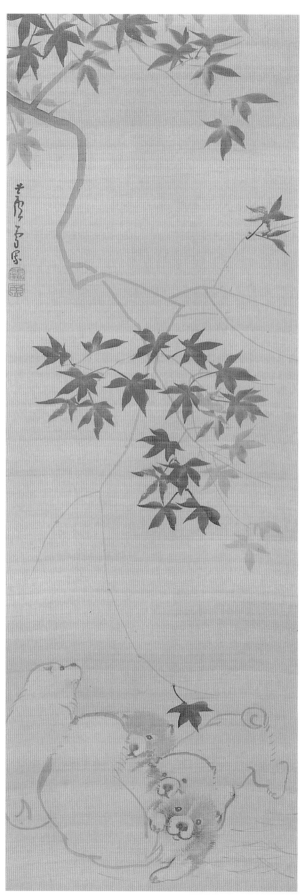

Water Jar
(Japan, Hirado kilns, Edo period, second half of the eighteenth century)
Porcelain decorated in underglaze blue, height 7 ³⁄₁₆ ins
(18.3 cm)
Bequest of Henry Walters, 1931; 49.283

This jar was made for use in the tea ceremony to hold
fresh water. Japanese porcelain manufacture—which
developed much later than that of China—flourished
on the island of Kyushu in the last decades of the
seventeenth century. The family-run Hirado kilns
were one of the few to produce innovative wares
of the highest quality in the eighteenth century.

Nagasawa Rosetsu
(Japan, Edo period, 1754-99)
Puppies under a Maple Branch
Ink and color on silk, 42 ½ x 14 ¼ ins (108 x 36.2 cm)
Bequest of Henry Walters, 1931; 35.74

When he painted this autumn scene, Nagasawa Rosetsu,
the son of a warrior, had become adept at the free
brushwork and playful compositions for which he is
renowned.

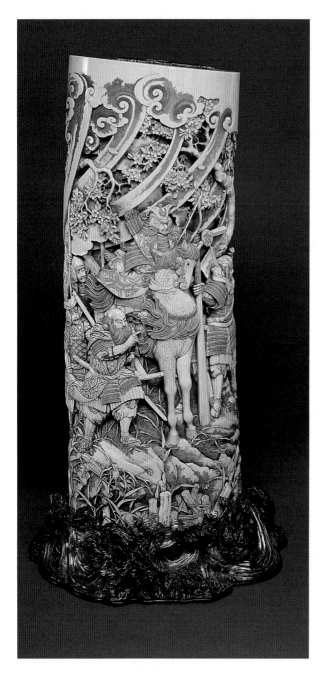

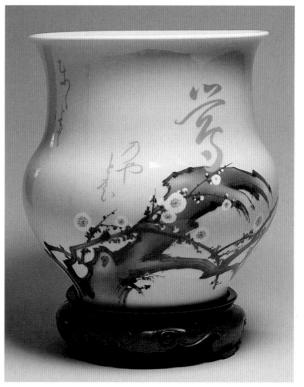

Miyagawa Kozan
(Japan, Meiji period, 1842-1916)
Vase with Blossoming Plum, c. 1904
Porcelain decorated with underglaze blue,
pink, and yellow, 12 ³⁄₁₆ ins (31 cm)
Bequest of Henry Walters, 1931; 49.1912

Around the year 950 the emperor received an
anonymous poem that made him change his
mind about removing an ancient plum tree that
had recently died: "Since my lord commands, what
can I do but obey; but the nightingales, when they
ask about their nests—whatever can I tell them?"
The character for "nightingale" is perched upon
the branch; amazingly, it (and the other characters)
consists of transparent clay, inserted into the cut-out
wall of the vessel.

Ishikawa Komei
(Japan, Meiji period, 1852-1913)
Vase with the Warrior Yoshitsune, c. 1880
Ivory, height 21 ⅛ ins (53.6 cm)
Bequest of Henry Walters, 1931; 71.1080

Mounted on a horse, the twelfth-century warrior
Yoshitsune, spurned by his brother—for whom
Yoshitsune's military prowess had secured the rulership
of Japan—prepared to leave the country by sea. But
stormy weather—the silver waves of the base—prevent
his departure. The vase is said to have been
commissioned by the Japanese government in a period
when the carvers of ivory *netsuke* were faced with the
loss of a market, due to the adoption of western dress.

Workshop of Kawasaki Jimbei II (overleaf)
(Japan, Meiji period, 1853-1910)
The Mongol Invasion, c. 1904
Silk tapestry, height 143 ⅝ ins (378 cm)
Bequest of Henry Walters, 1931; 82.25

The Mongols invaded Japan twice, in 1274 and 1281,
and twice they were repulsed with the help of a sudden
typhoon (a *kamikaze* or "divine wind"). Kawasaki
Jimbei II began to produce large-scale silk tapestries
following his visit to France in 1886. This tapestry
was based on a full-size oil painting by Morizumo
Yugyo (1854-1927).

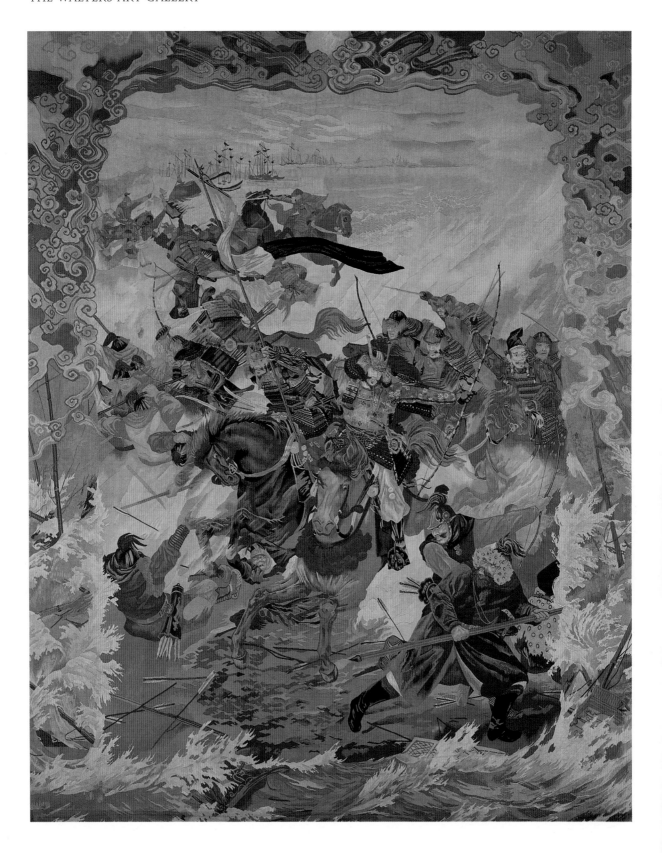

Islamic Art

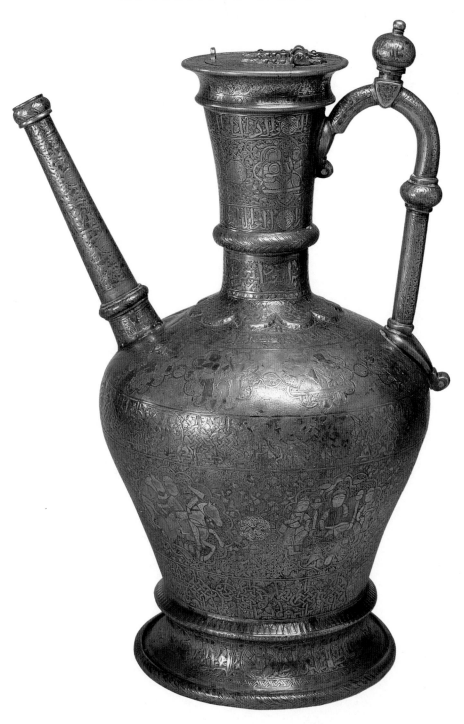

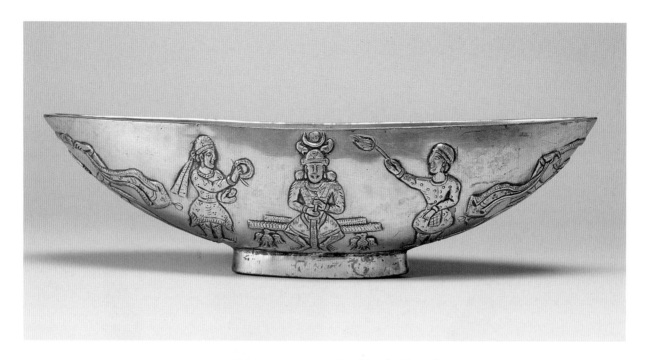

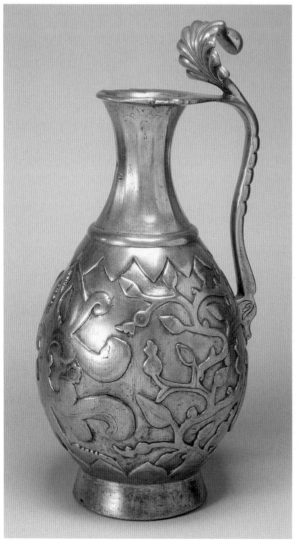

Oval Bowl with Enthronement Scene

(Iran, seventh century or later)
Silver, 3 x 10 ⁷⁄₁₆ ins (7.6 x 26.5 cm)
Bequest of Henry Walters, 1931; 57.625

The enthroned king in the center of this hammered and carved bowl is flanked on the right by an attendant waving a fly whisk and on the left by a noble or princely figure holding a beaded diadem. The ends of the bowl are adorned with dancing girls, whose long scarfs fly back toward the central scene. Although long associated with silver vessels made in Iran during the Sassanian dynasty (224–651 AD), the shape and decoration suggest that The Walters bowl dates from the early Islamic era.

Ewer

(Iran, eighth-ninth century)
Brass with copper inlay, height 14 ⁹⁄₁₆ ins (37 cm)
Bequest of Henry Walters, 1931; 54.457

This handsome object exemplifies a group of cast brass ewers believed to be among the earliest known examples of Islamic metalwork. It is distinguished by its pear-shaped body, elegant palmette handle, and vegetal designs in bold relief.

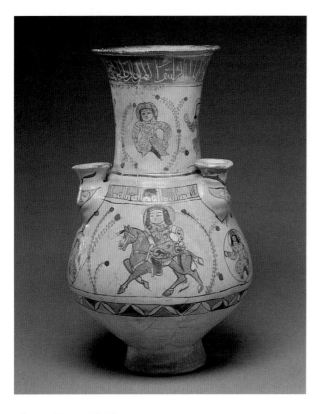

Flower Vase with Horsemen
(Iran, thirteenth century)
Overglaze-painted enamel and lustreware,
height 8 ¹⁵⁄₁₆ ins (22.7 cm)
Bequest of Henry Walters, 1931; 48.1278

While the combination of enamel (or *mina'i*) and lustre painted decoration is somewhat unusual, riders and seated figures are commonly represented together on medieval Islamic ceramics.

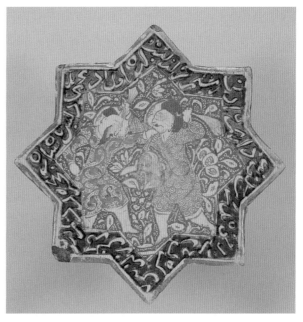

Star Tile with Combat Scene
(Iran, late thirteenth-fourteenth century)
Underglaze-painted and overglaze lustreware,
diameter 8 ⅛ ins (20.6 cm)
Bequest of Henry Walters, 1931; 48.1288

The Persian verses written around the outer blue band come from the *Shahnama* (Book of Kings), the national epic of Iran, and specifically from a section of the text that recounts the tragic combat between the great hero Rustam and his son Sohrab. It is unlikely, however, that the two men fighting in the center of this tile are meant to illustrate the *Shahnama* text.

Plate
(Iran, Nishapur, dated 885/1480-81)
Underglaze-painted fritware, diameter 14 ¾ ins (37.5 cm)
Bequest of Henry Walters, 1931; 48.1031

This plate is one of a few rare dated ceramics from the Timurid period. Scientific testing of its fabric demonstrates that it came from Nishapur, a town in northeastern Iran that flourished as a ceramic-manufacturing center in the ninth-twelfth centuries and that is now recognized—partly on the basis of the evidence provided by our plate—to have remained active in pottery production during subsequent periods.

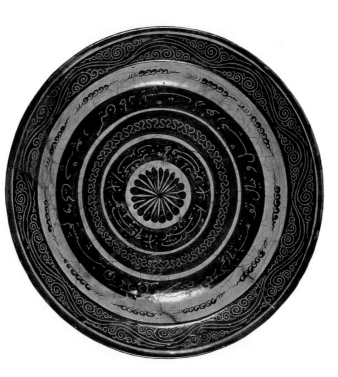

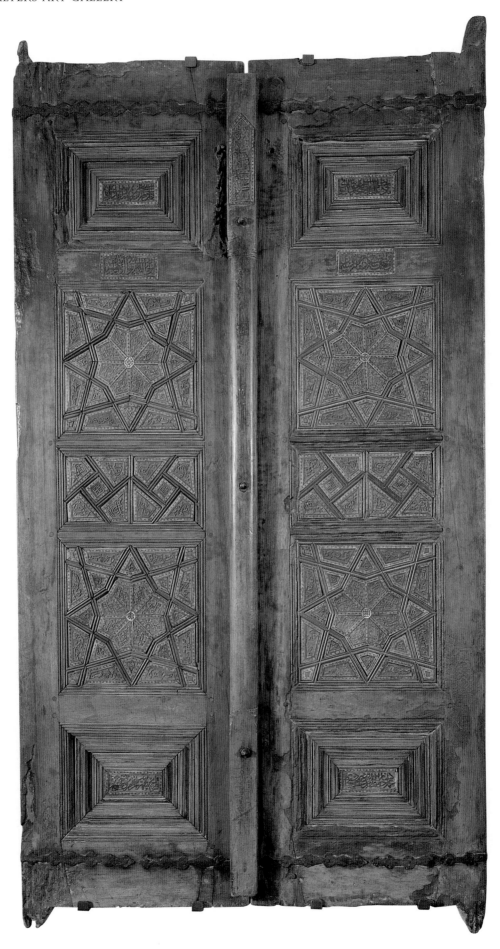

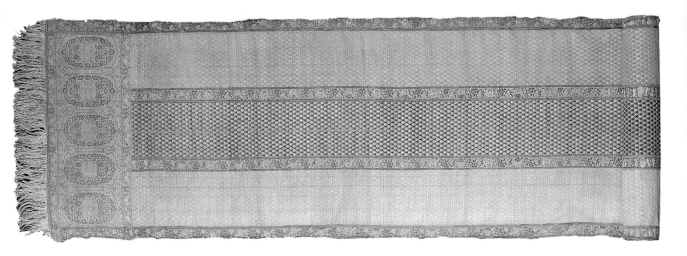

Mausoleum Doors (opposite)
(Iran, Qanbar ibn Mahmud, dated Muharram 959/December 1551-January 1552)
Wood inlaid with ivory, 74 ³⁄₁₆ x 40 ½ ins (188.5 x 102.8 cm)
Bequest of Henry Walters, 1931; 61.297

The original placement of these doors in a tomb explains their decorative program, including panels with radiating star designs that evoke the eternal and inscriptions in praise of Ali, son-in-law of the Prophet Muhammad and the leader of Shi'ite Islam, which became the state religion in sixteenth-century Iran. The maker's full name, carved in the lower right panel, indicates that he was the son of a carpenter and confirms that crafts such as woodcarving were practiced by generations within the same family.

Sash
(Iran or India, seventeenth-eighteenth century)
Gold and silver brocade, 180 ¹¹⁄₁₆ x 23 ⅜ ins (459 x 59.4 cm)
Bequest of Henry Walters, 1931; 83.14

This long sash would have been folded lengthwide and wrapped many times around its wearer's outer robe. The decoration of the narrow bands running along the top, bottom, and middle includes small male figures in the style of contemporary miniature painting.

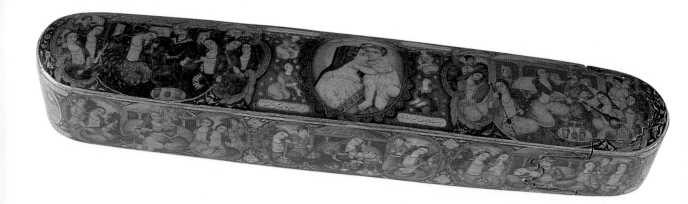

Muhammad Isma'il

(Iran, active 1840s-70s)

Penbox with Scenes of Bahram Gur and the Madonna and Child, dated 1283/1866-67

Lacquerwork (painted and varnished papier-mâché),
1 ⁹⁄₁₆ ins x 9 ³⁄₁₆ (4 cm x 23.4)
Bequest of Henry Walters, 1931; 67.3

Muhammad Isma'il was a member of a family of nineteenth-century Iranian lacquer painters noted for their delicate and complex style. On this penbox the artist has combined traditional scenes of the amorous adventures of the Sassanian King Bahram Gur, drawn from classical Persian poetry, and a Christian image of the Madonna and Child which was probably modeled on a western European print.

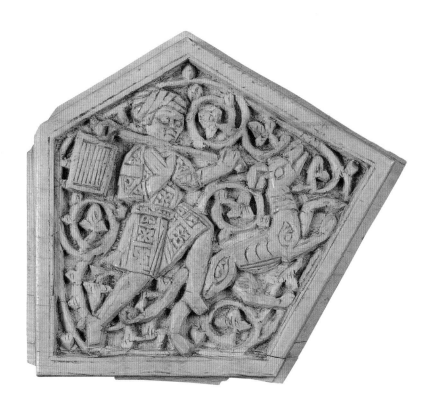

Carved Panel with Man and Dog
(Egypt, eleventh-twelfth century)
Ivory, 2 ⅞ x 3 ⅝ ins (7.3 x 9.1 cm)
Bequest of Henry Walters, 1931; 71.562

This panel probably formed part of the decorative inlay of a piece of furniture. The animation of the running figures is typical of Islamic art in Egypt during the Fatimid period (909–1171), when objects of all kinds were decorated with very realistic representations.

Candlestick Base
(Egypt, c. 1290)
Brass inlaid with silver, gold and copper,
height 10 ¼ ins (26 cm),
diameter 12 ¹³⁄₁₆ ins (32.5 cm)
Bequest of Henry Walters, 1931; 54.459

Both the candlestick base and the neck (in the Museum of Islamic Art, Cairo) are inscribed with the name of Zayn al-Din Kitbugha, who served as *saqi* or cupbearer at the court of the Mamluk dynasty in Eygpt before ascending the throne in 1294. The large inscription in *thuluth* script around the candlestick's body is punctuated by roundels featuring a stemmed cup, the blazon of Kitbugha's office before he became sultan.

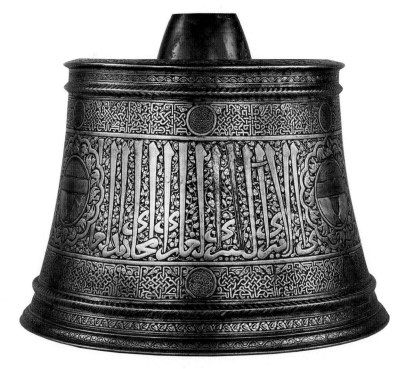

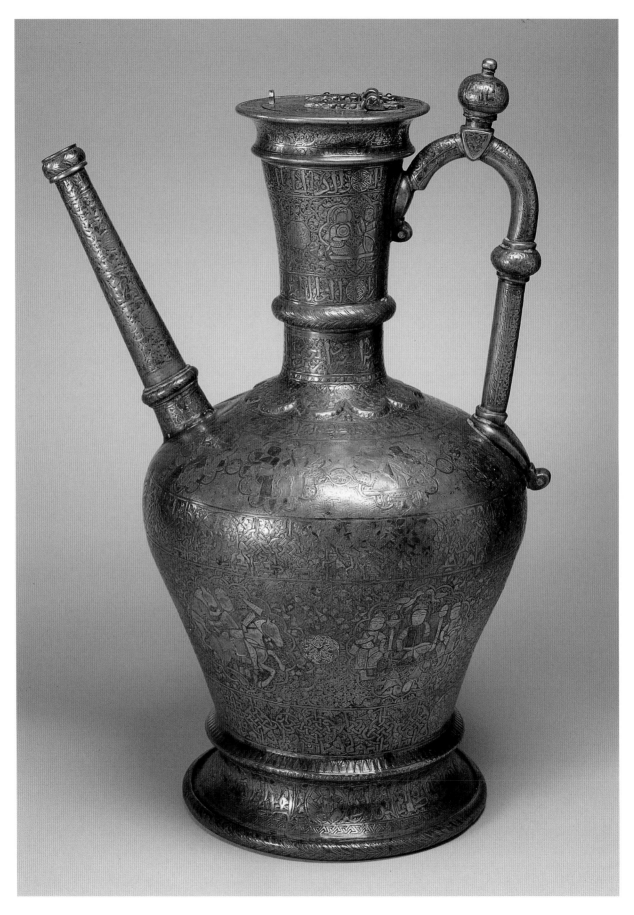

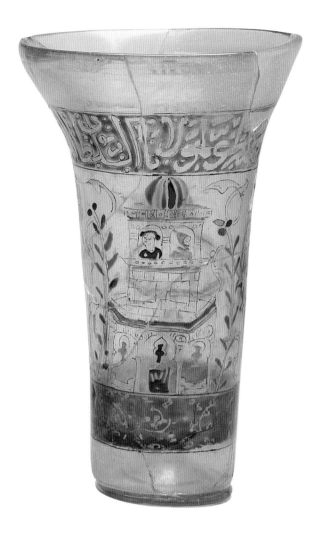

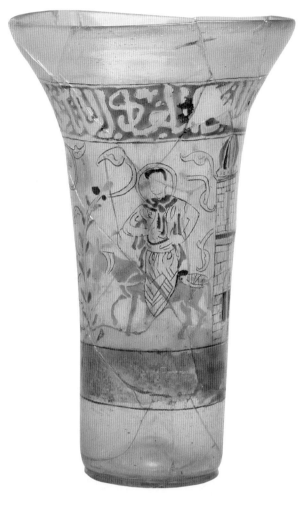

**Yunus ibn Yusuf al-naqqash ("the decorator")
al-Mawsili (opposite)**
(Iraq or Syria, thirteenth century)
Ewer, dated 644/1246-47
Brass inlaid with silver, height 17 ⁹⁄₁₆ ins (44.6 cm)
Bequest of Henry Walters, 1931; 54.456

The richly decorated surface of this ewer features
multiple bands of Arabic inscriptions and scalloped
medallions enclosing musicians, enthroned figures,
hunters, and other scenes characteristic of medieval
Islamic art. Although the artist who executed the dense
inlaid designs has signed his name al-Mawsili, meaning
"from Mosul," a town in northern Iraq, he could just
as easily have been working in Syria, where metal
workshops produced vessels of similar form and
decor during the thirteenth century.

Pair of Beakers (above)
(Syria, c. 1260)
Gilded and enameled glass, height: 47.17: 7 ⁵⁄₁₆ ins (18.5 cm) and
47.18: 6 ¹¹⁄₁₆ ins (17 cm)
Bequest of Henry Walters, 1931; 47.17 and 47.18

The two works, perhaps made as a set, date from
the Crusader period when Islamic imagery, including
inscriptions in Arabic, as here, was often combined
with Christian themes. Both include compositions
in which figures resembling saints alternate with
two-storied, domed structures that may represent
monastic communities. The smaller vessel (47.18)
also depicts a figure riding a white donkey—possibly
Christ entering Jerusalem.

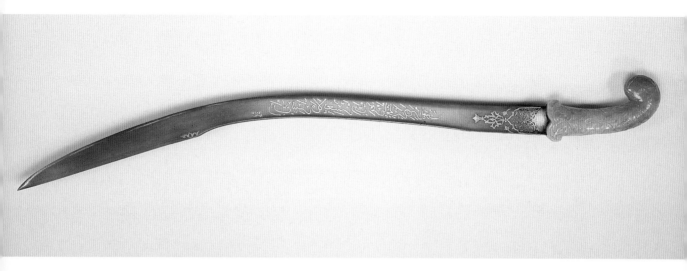

Hajji Salim
(Turkey, Trebizond, eighteenth century)
Kilij, dated 1175/1761
Replacement grip, India, seventeenth-eighteenth century
Steel decorated with gold, jade grip, length 29 ¾ ins
(76.6 cm)
Bequest of Henry Walters, 1931; 51.14

The *kilij* is a Turkish development of the saber and
was used for thrusting rather than slicing. The gold
inscription across the blade, which is oriented upside
down to the cutting edge, invokes God's favor and
assistance. This work belongs to The Walters'
extensive collection of Islamic arms and armor.

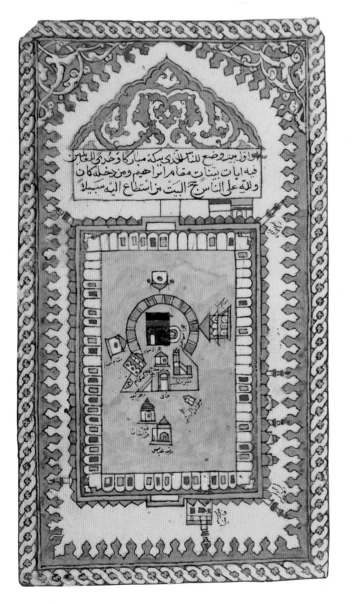

Tile with the Great Mosque of Mecca
(Turkey, seventeenth century)
Underglaze-painted fritware, 24 ⁹⁄₁₆ x 14 ⅛ ins
(62.4 x 35.8 cm)
Bequest of Henry Walters, 1931; 48.1307

The three lines of Arabic writing in the upper part of
the tile are from the third chapter of the Koran, and
exhort the Muslim faithful to make the pilgrimage
to Mecca. The rest of the tile is given over to a
bird's-eye representation of the Great Mosque in
Mecca, with the Ka'ba, Islam's holiest shrine, in
the center surrounded by various other structures,
all identified in Arabic, and a rectangular portico
around the courtyard.

Manuscripts & Rare Books

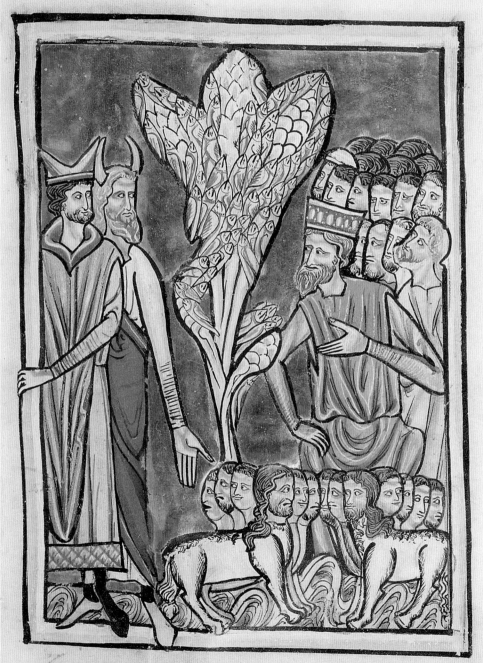

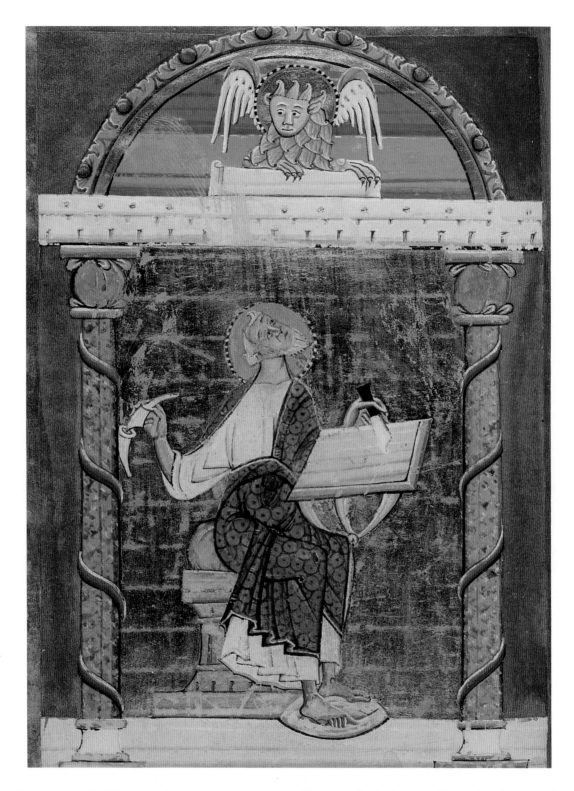

Gospel Book: Portrait of the Evangelist Mark
(Southern German, Reichenau(?), c. 1040-70)
Tempera on vellum, 9 1/16 x 6 9/16 ins (23 x 16.6 cm)
Bequest of Henry Walters, 1931; MS W.7, folio 67v

Probably produced in the well-known Benedictine abbey
on the island of Reichenau, this graceful miniature in a
Gospel book shows St. Mark about to begin writing.

The Evangelist looks up to his symbol, the winged
lion, for inspiration as he dips his quill in a horn inkwell
and holds the page down with a penknife. The purple
color imitates the luxury books that were written in
gold on purple-stained vellum in the times of late
antiquity. The architectural setting, and Mark's
tunic and toga, are similarly inspired by the art
of the Roman Empire.

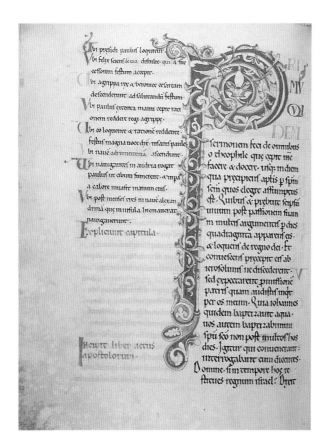

New Testament: Initial to the Acts of the Apostles
(English, Rochester, c. 1130-40)
Tempera on vellum, 14 ⁹⁄₁₆ x 10 ¹³⁄₁₆ ins (37 x 27.4 cm)
Bequest of Henry Walters, 1931; MS W.18, folio 107v

This book was once part of a complete multi-volume
Bible copied and used at the monastic priory of
Rochester Cathedral. As was often the case in the
high Romanesque period, large initials formed the
exclusive focus of the illuminator's decorative
fantasy. The dragons and spiralling plant scrolls
of the monumental initial "P" were much in vogue
in England and northern France in the twelfth century.
Simple initials in different colored inks enliven the
list of chapters, which ends in the left-hand column.

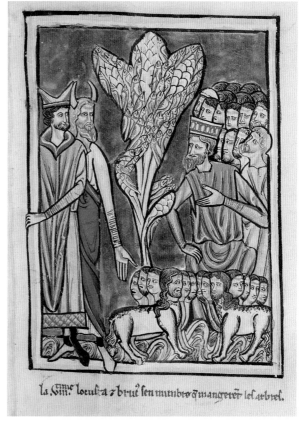

William de Brailes
(English, Oxford, active 1230s-40s)
The Plague of Locusts, c. 1230s-40s
Tempera on vellum, 5 ⅛ x 3 ¹⁵⁄₁₆ ins (13 x 10 cm)
Bequest of Henry Walters, 1931; MS W.106, folio 9

One of only two English thirteenth-century illuminators
known by name, William de Brailes was an inventive
artist with a distinctive, quirky style. This illustration
is one of an extensive series of biblical scenes, now
incomplete, that may once have prefaced a psalter or
prayer book. The image of the eighth plague shows
locusts devouring a tree while others appear as
human-headed quadrupeds at Pharaoh's feet. Moses
(horned, at left) gestures a dramatic warning to the
seated monarch as he and Aaron turn to leave. The
hand and feet resting on the frame of the miniature
add a dynamic immediacy to their departure.

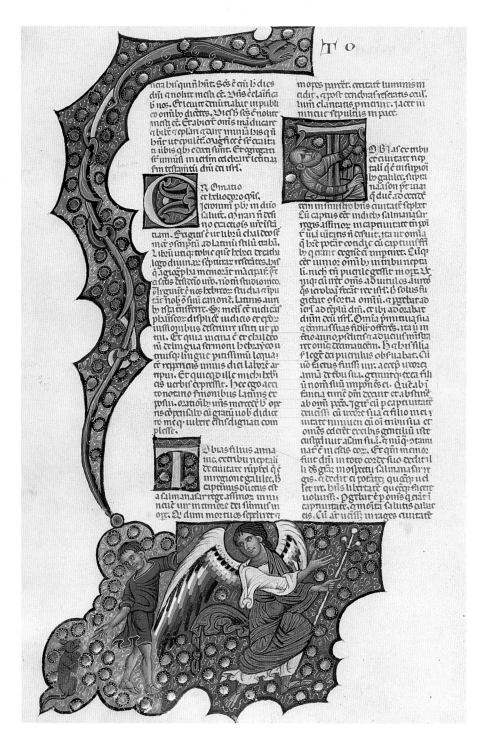

The Conradin Bible: Tobias and the Angel
(Italian, c. 1265)
Tempera and gold leaf on parchment, 14 ¼ x 9 ¹³⁄₁₆ ins
(36.2 x 25 cm)
Bequest of Henry Walters, 1931; MS W.152, folio 156v

A remarkable, fragmentary Bible has long been
associated with the young Conradin, King of Jerusalem
and Sicily and last of the Hohenstaufen dynasty, who
was beheaded in Naples in 1268 at the age of sixteen.
Of particular interest in the folio here is the combination
of Byzantine and western characteristics. The strong
sense of volume and the deeply modeled facial features
of the figures are clearly borrowed from the eastern
Mediterranean, whereas the placement of biblical
scenes in cusped fields of marginal decoration is more
characteristic of western Europe.

Also quintessentially western is the apparent
spontaneity and tenderness of expression depicted in the
archangel leading Tobias and the boy holding on to his
guide's wing with one hand as he beckons his dog with
the other.

The Beaupré Antiphonary (Volume I):
Musician Angels; Harrowing of Hell
(Flemish, dated 1290)
Vellum, 18 ¹⁵⁄₁₆ x 13 ⅝ ins (48.1 x 34.6 cm)
Gift of the Hearst Foundation, 1957; MS W.759, folio 2, detail

Once bound in six volumes, this masterpiece of Gothic
illumination was commissioned by a woman of the
Viane family for the Cistercian convent of Beaupré. The
initial large "A" for "Alleluia" that opens the Easter vigils
depicts Christ's descent into Hell after his Crucifixion to
free the souls of the righteous, to whom Heaven was
now open. The tall, slender figure of Christ stands on the
Devil, vanquished and in chains, as he leads Adam and
Eve and a crowd of others out of a gaping hell-mouth.
A small demon still threatens atop the monstrous snout.
In the upper register, three graceful angels celebrate by
playing a harp, a fiddle, and a portable organ. Burlesque
marginal figures above were erased in a less tolerant era.

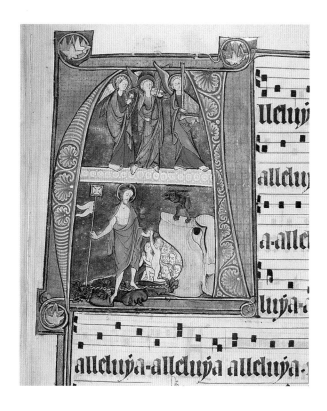

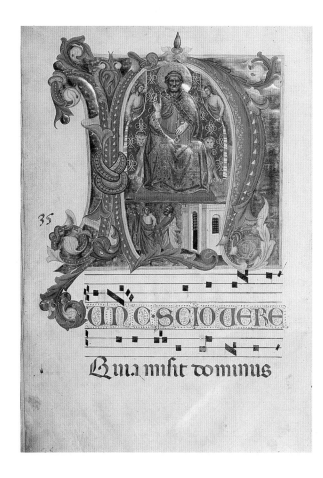

Cenni di Francesco
(Italian, Florence, active 1370s-1410s)
Antiphonary-Gradual: Saint Peter Enthroned; Peter Freed
from Prison by the Angel, c. 1380
Tempera and gold on parchment, 23 ¹³⁄₁₆ x 16 ⅞ ins
(60.5 x 41.8 cm)
Bequest of Henry Walters, 1931; MS W.153, folio 35v

The large initial "N" illustrated in this grandiose choir-
book presents St. Peter, his hand raised in blessing and
seated majestically upon a stool decorated with lions'
heads. The Florentine painter Cenni di Francesco has
painted Peter's cope directly on to a field of burnished
gold. This unusual technique adds to the sumptuous
appearance of the drapery and complements the rich
acanthus ornament of the initial itself.

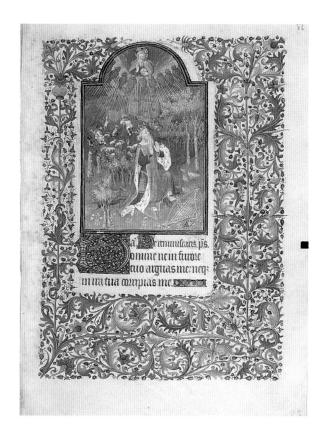

Master of the Harvard Hannibal and Associates
(French, Paris, active 1410-30)
**Book of Hours: David in Prayer in a Landscape,
  c. 1420-30**
Tempera on vellum, 9 ⅟₁₆ x 6 ¹¹⁄₁₆ ins (23 x 17)
Bequest of Henry Walters, 1931; MS W.287, folio 86

The delicate, painterly style of this image exemplifies
the best of Parisian illumination in the first half of the
fifteenth century. The landscape receding into the
distance was a relative novelty at that time. The
owners of luxury prayer books enjoyed incidental
details such as the shepherds and their flock on the
hillside and the individually detailed flowers. The
acanthus ornament in the border is especially lush.

Willem Vrelant and Associates
(Flemish, Bruges, active 1450-60)
**Book of Hours: Owner Presented to Christ
by St. Catherine, c. 1450**
Tempera on vellum, 5 ⅞ x 3 ¹⁵⁄₁₆ ins
(15 x 10 cm)
Bequest of Henry Walters, 1931; MS W.220,
folio 150v

This private devotional book was apparently made
for a married couple. Here the neatly dressed
female owner of the manuscript kneels on the tiled
floor of a room; her patron saint, recognizable by
her crown and a piece of the wheel on which she
was tortured as St. Catherine, presents the woman
to Christ enthroned. The clarity and precision of
the draftsmanship characterize the early style of
Willem Vrelant. The graceful border ornament may
reflect French influence.

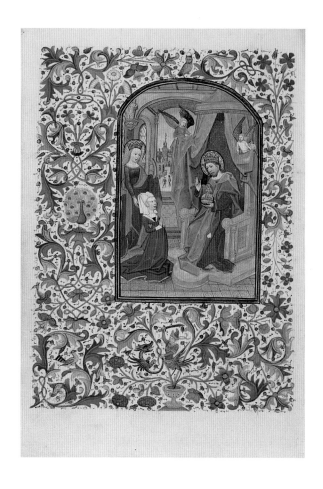

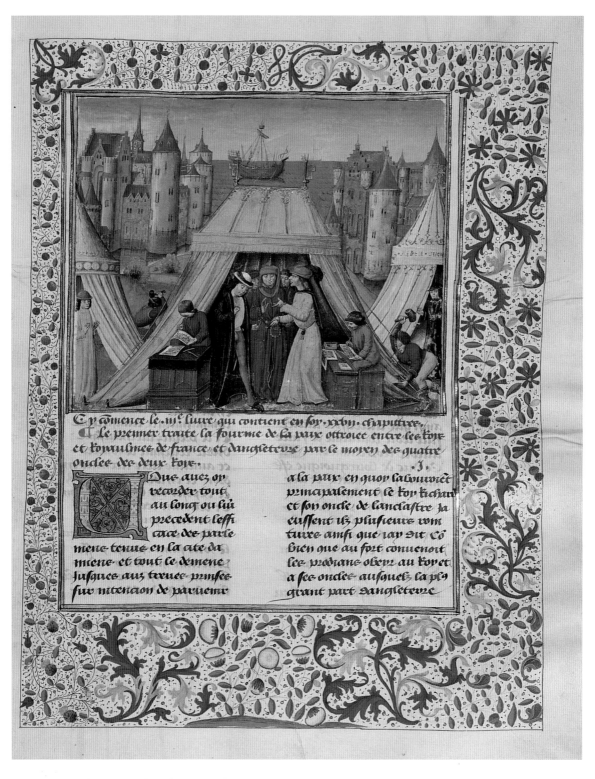

Jean de Wavrin, Chroniques d'Angleterre (Volume IV): Negotiations for a Peace Treaty

(Flemish, Ghent(?), c. 1475-80)
Tempera on vellum, 16 ¹⁵⁄₁₆ x 13 ⅜ ins (43 x 34 cm)
Bequest of Henry Walters, 1931; MS W.201, folio 147

On the opening page of the third section of this volume of the Chronicles of England, members of the English and French royal families negotiate a treaty that marked a temporary truce in the Hundred Years' War. Scribes record the terms of the agreement. The date is 1395 and the location is a tent pitched in neutral territory between the fortified cities of Calais and Boulogne, seen in the background. An English galley rides at anchor off shore. Flemish painters in the later fifteenth century increasingly favored the naturalistic style in evidence here.

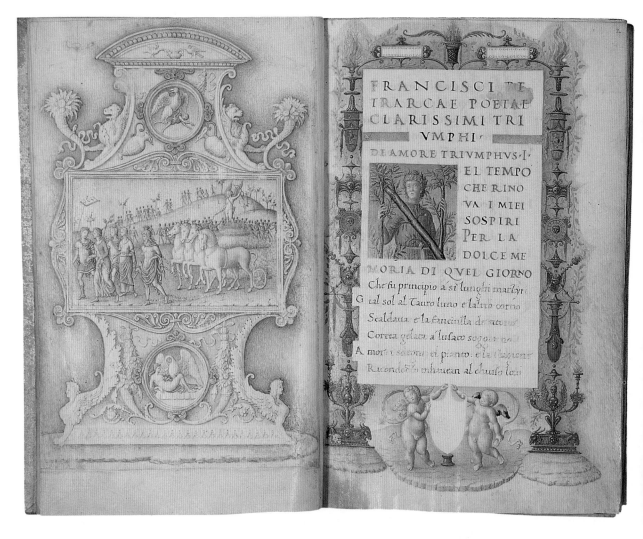

Francesco Petrarch, I Trionfi (The Triumphs):
The Triumph of Love
(Italian, Rome and Florence, c. 1480)
Copied by Bartolomeo Sanvito, 1435-1518
Vellum, 8 ⁷⁄₁₆ x 5 ⅜ ins (21.5 x 13.6 cm)
Museum Purchase, 1955; MS W.755, folio 1v–2

The illuminated openings of the first two Triumphs in
this allegorical poem by Petrarch (1504–74) are Paduan in
style. Current scholarship suggests that they may have
been painted by Sanvito himself, as the artist's hand
appears in at least ten of the manuscripts he copied.
The influence of Andrea Mantegna (1431–1506) is
apparent in the style of the figures and in the abundant
use of ornamental motifs of classical origin, such as the
sphinxes, urns, acanthus, garlands, and cornucopias seen
here. Images delicately shaded in pale tones within a
fanciful architectural frame evoke ancient marble
sculpture in low relief.

Book of Hours: Flight into Egypt (opposite)
(Flemish, Bruges (?) c. 1510)
Tempera on vellum, 3 ¾ x 2 ½ ins (9.5 x 6.5 cm)
Bequest of Henry Walters, 1931; MS W.427, folios 115v–116

This delicate book of hours provides a fine example of
Flemish illumination in the early sixteenth century. The
miniature seems to open out behind the surface of the
page into a naturalistic landscape across which the Holy
Family travels. The peaceful atmosphere of the scene and
many of its details find parallels throughout the work of
Simon Bening. The fresh flowers and insects strewn
throughout the gold borders serve a symbolic as well as
a decorative purpose: the sharp-leaved iris alludes to
Mary's sorrow at her son's death, and butterflies and
moths stand for Christ's Resurrection.

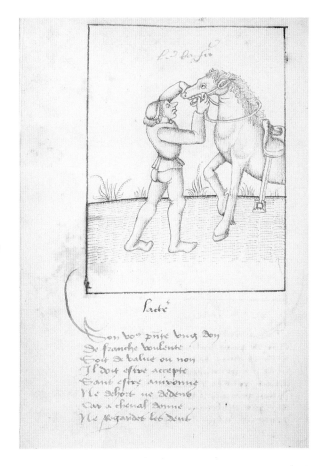

Proverbes en rimes (Rhyming proverbs):
Don't Look a Gift Horse in the Mouth
(French, Savoy, c. 1480)
Ink on paper, 7 ⅞ x 5 ⅛ ins (20 x 13 cm)
Bequest of Henry Walters, 1931; MS W.313, folio 17v

Proverbes en rimes is a rare survival of a type of secular book made to appeal to middle-class tastes and pockets. Each illustration in this modest manuscript functions as a riddle or charade to which the stanza below provides the answer. The drawings give a literal illustration of a saying, in this case an expression still in use in English today in the same form. The text provides clues to the hidden meaning, followed by the actual saying at the end.

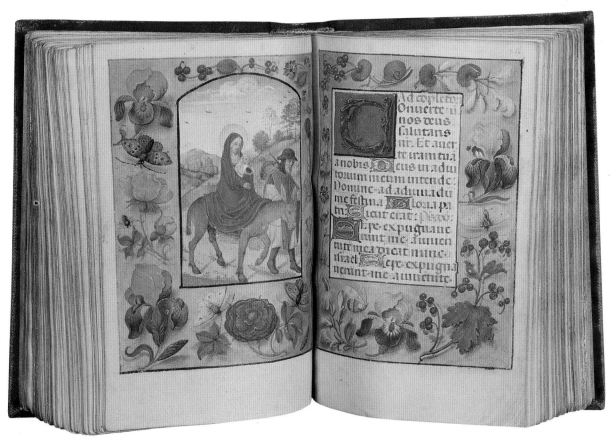

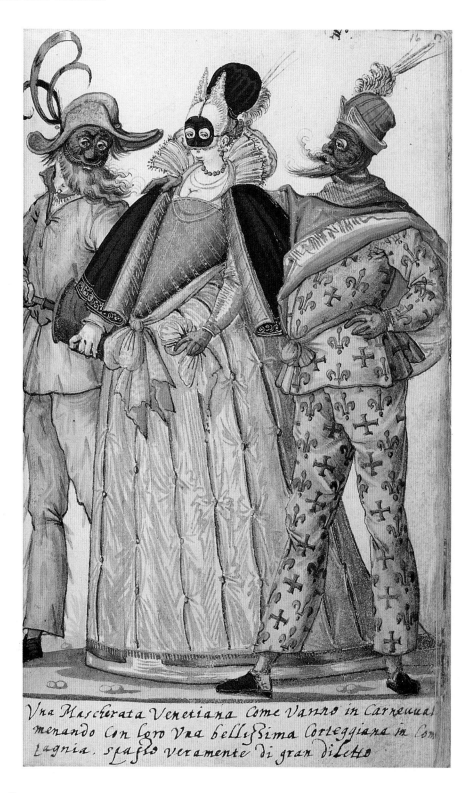

Vna Mascherata Venetiana Come Vanno in Carneual
menando Con loro Vna bellissima Corteggiana in Com
pagnia, spasso veramente di gran diletto

Niclauss Kippell
(Italian, Venice or Padua)
Costume Book: Venetian Carnival Revellers, c. 1588
Tempera on paper, 5 ^{11}/$_{16}$ x 3 ^{9}/$_{16}$ ins (14.5 x 9 cm)
Bequest of Henry Walters, 1931; MS W.477, folio 16

Kippell was probably from Germany. He painted this
volume of a collection of costumes from Venice and
other Italian cities as a souvenir of his visit to Italy.
Twenty years later Kippell presented the book to his
friend Beat Hagenbach of Basel. The watercolors depict
Italians from various walks of life. Especially colorful are
these masked carnival revellers, two men with flowing
beards and an elegant courtesan.

118

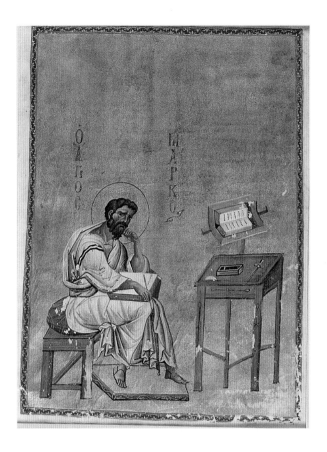

Leaf from a Gospel Book: The Evangelist Mark in his Study

(Byzantine, Constantinople, late tenth century)
Vellum, 10 ½ x 7 ½ ins (26.5 x 19 cm)
Bequest of Henry Walters, 1931; MS W.530a

Painted in the finest manner of the court circles of Constantinople, this miniature is based on ancient portraits of philosopher-writers: Mark has written a few words on his blank page and pauses, lost in thought. The deep, stylized modeling of the face creates a feeling of intensity. The proportions and dress of the figure are inherited from classical antiquity. On the sloping desk at the right lie an inkwell and a compass beneath the book cradled on a lectern.

Imperial Menologion for January: Life of the Prophet Micah

(Byzantine, Constantinople, c. 1040)
Vellum, 11 ⅝ x 9 ½ ins (29.7 x 23.6 cm)
Bequest of Henry Walters, 1931; MS W.521, folio 36

The manuscript is known as a menologion, from the Greek for "month." It was written and illuminated in the imperial scriptorium in Constantinople, and is one of the few editions to be so richly illustrated. It is a collection of the lives of the saints honored in January and is arranged by the days of the liturgical year on which each saint is venerated. Seen here is the martyrdom of the prophet Micah; he is about to be pushed off a craggy cliff at the left and subsequently entombed by his followers at the right.

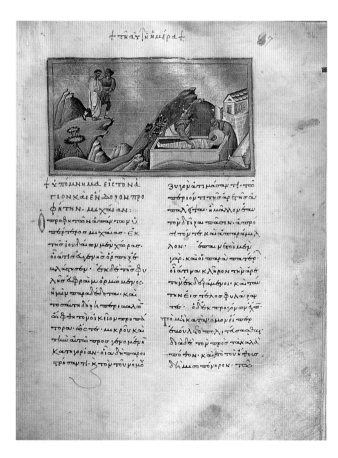

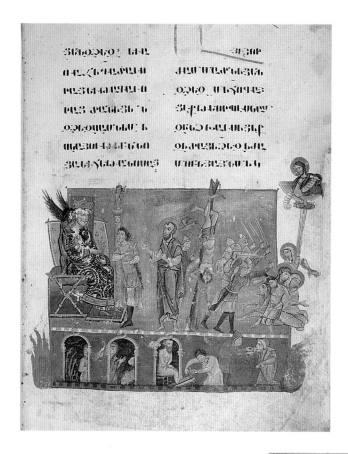

T'oros Roslin
(Cilician Armenia, Hromkla, active mid-thirteenth century)
Gospel Book: Christ Predicting the Sufferings of His Followers, 1262
Tempera on parchment, 7 11/16 x 5 1/2 ins (19.5 x 14 cm)
Bequest of Mrs. Henry Walters, 1935; MS W.539, folio 48

T'oros Roslin, scribe of this Gospel as well as master of its exquisite miniatures, fused Armenian, Byzantine, and western elements to create his own unique style of illumination. One of the finest and most densely illustrated of Roslin's seven signed manuscripts, the volume was made at Hromkla, Cilicia (formerly part of Armenia and now in southern Turkey), for T'oros the Priest, nephew of the Catholicos (patriarch) of the Armenian Church. On this page Christ, appearing in the margin at the upper right, prophesies the persecution and suffering of his followers (Matthew 10:16-23), as carried out by the king enthroned at the left with a devil whispering in his ear.

Khatchatur
(Greater Armenia, Lake Van region, active mid-fifteenth century)
Gospel Book: The Sacrifice of Isaac, 1455
Vellum, 10 13/16 x 7 1/16 ins (27.5 x 18 cm)
Bequest of Henry Walters, 1931; MS W.543, folio 4

The only known work of the artist Khatchatur displays a remarkable boldness in the use of line, color, and overall design. Abraham, dynamically poised to slit his son's throat, is interrupted by an angel in swirling robes, who points to the ram with a finger almost as long and sharp as the deadly knife. The animal is separated from the other figures by the wavy diagonal of a fantastic tree. Like the elongated eyes of the characters, the decorative foliage is inspired by contemporary Persian art.

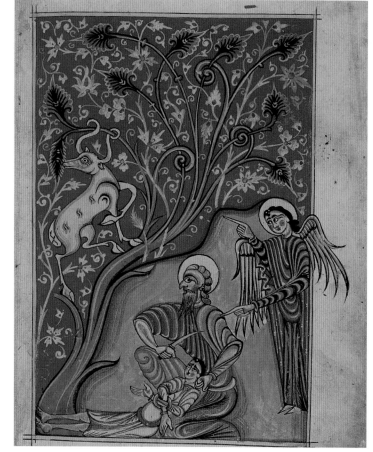

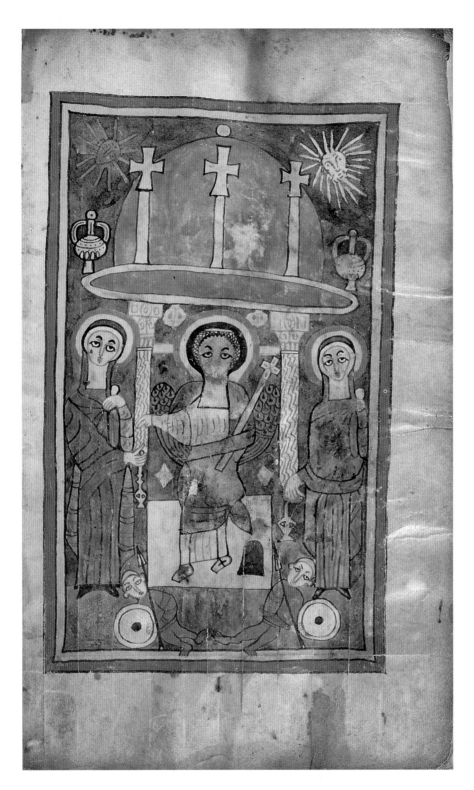

Gospel Book: The Women at the Tomb
(Northern Ethiopia, early fourteenth century)
Tempera on parchment, 10 ½ x 6 ½ ins (26.6 x 16.5 cm)
Museum Purchase through the W. Alton Jones Foundation
Acquisition Fund, 1996; MS W.836, folio 7

This is one of a family of Gospel books produced at a
monastery in northern Ethiopia sometime during the

fourteenth century. This folio, one of three prefatory
miniatures, shows the two Marys who have come to
the tomb of Christ to anoint his body; they are greeted
by an angel with news of Christ's Resurrection. The
setting is based on Byzantine cult imagery probably
introduced into Ethiopian art during the sixth century.
It represents the Holy Sepulcher in Jerusalem as it
appeared to be at that time.

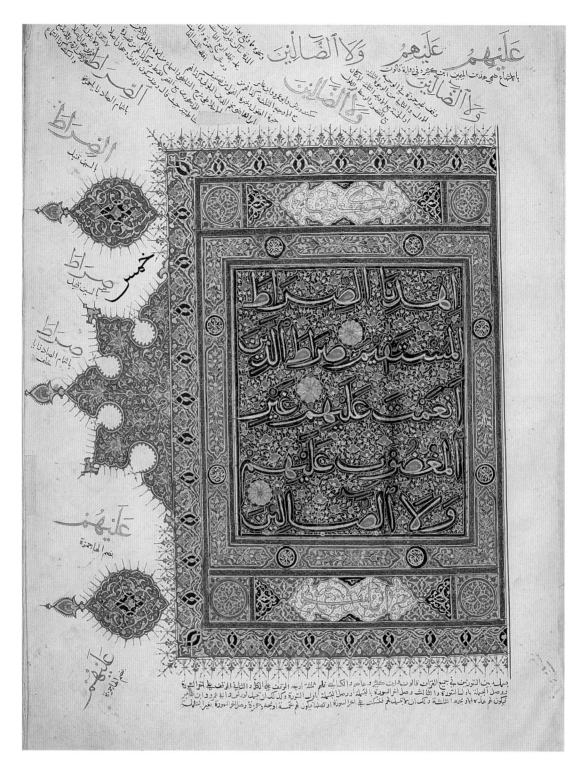

Koran: Illuminated Folio with Sura (Chapter) 2
(Northern India (?), fifteenth century)
Tempera and gold on paper, 15 ⁹⁄₁₆ x 12 ½ ins
(39.5 x 31.7 cm)
Bequest of Henry Walters, 1931; MS W.563, folio 9

A series of richly decorated folios that enframe the first chapters of the holy text open this sumptuous copy of the Koran. Although previously attributed to Iran's fifteenth-century Timurid period, the style of the illumination, including the dense profusion of gold blossoms, the distinctive color scheme (featuring black and mauve), and the large scalloped projection at the side, has now been recognized as probably being of Indian origin. The inscriptions in the margins are commentaries done by both contemporary and later readers of the manuscript.

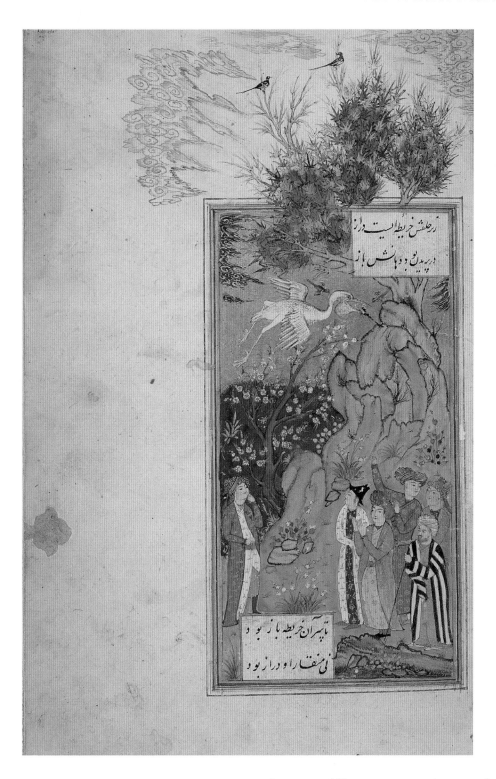

***Shaykh Azari*, Ghara'ib al-Dunya (Marvels of the World):
A Crowd Watches a Flying Pelican Luring Smaller Birds
into its Large Beak**
(Iran, Herat, dated 22 Rajab 1022/8 September 1613)
Tempera and gold on paper, 11 ¾ x 6 ¾ ins (30 x 17.2 cm)
Bequest of Henry Walters, 1931; MS W.652, folio 162

This manuscript was made for the library of Husayn
Khan Shamlu, an important patron and military leader
who governed Khurasan province (now mainly in
Iran) from 1598 to 1618. Although created in Herat
(in present-day Afghanistan), its fourteen illustrations
reflect the painting style favored at the Iranian capital
of Isfahan during the reign of the great Safavid ruler
Shah Abbas (reigned 1585–1628). Among the natural
phenomena depicted in this wonderful composition
is the human face incorporated into the mauve rock
formation in the center.

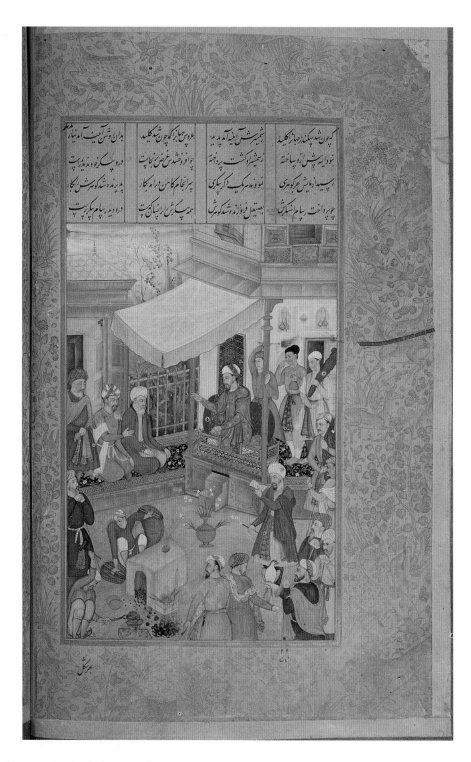

Nizami, **Iskandarnama (Book of Alexander):**
Iskandar supervises the Making of Mirrors
(India, Lahore, now Pakistan, dated 24 Azhar of Akbar's fortieth
regnal year/ 14 December 1595)
Copied by Abd al-Rahim "Ambarin Qalam" (amber pen),
illustration attributed to Nanha (active 1567–1604)
Tempera and gold on paper, 13 5/16 x 8 3/16 ins
(33.8 x 20.8 cm)
Bequest of Henry Walters, 1931; MS W.613, folio 16v

According to the twelfth-century poet Nizami, it was the
hero Iskandar (Alexander the Great) who introduced the
art of mirror-making to the world. In this right side to
a double-page composition, Iskandar discusses mirror
production with his advisors while the master ironsmith
Rassam directs the workforce. A young man with large
bellows tends a forge as an artisan shapes a round
mirror with a hammer and anvil. The rest of this Nizami
manuscript, which was made for the Mughal Emperor
Akbar (1542–1605), is in the British Library, London.

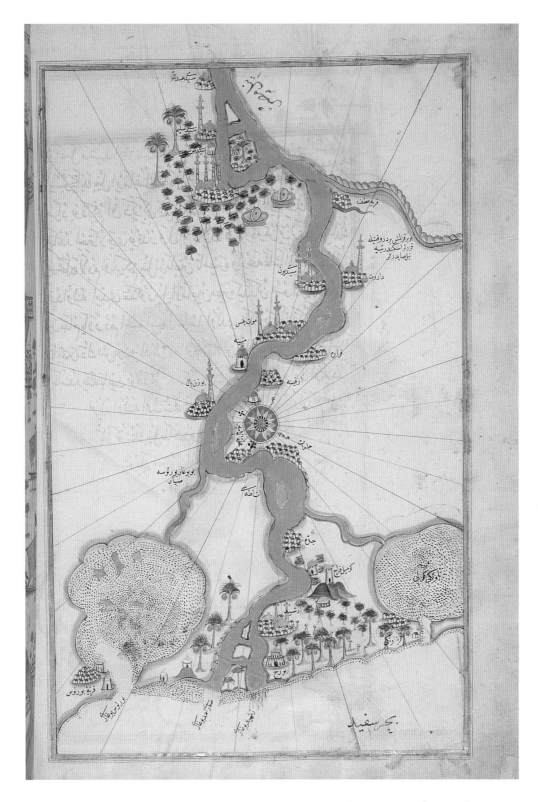

Piri Reis, Kitab-i Bahriye (Book of Maritime Matters): Map of the Nile Delta
(Turkey, seventeenth century)
Tempera, gold and ink on paper, 13 ⁷⁄₁₆ x 9 ½ ins
(34.3 x 23.5 cm)
Bequest of Henry Walters, 1931; MS W.658, folio 304v

Piri Reis (1465-1554) was a famous Ottoman cartographer and naval commander. This splendid copy of his maritime atlas describes the coasts, islands, and harbors of the Mediterranean. The map shown here depicts the east branch of the Nile delta in Egypt, with Lake Burullus and Lake Manzala. The largest of the towns near the mouth is the port of Damietta.

Bartholomaeus de Glanvilla, Anglicus,
Van den Proprieteyten der Dinghen
(On the Properties of Things): The Ages of Man
(Netherlandish, Haarlem, Jakob Bellaert, 1485)
Ink on paper with watercolor washes, 10 ¼ x 7 ¾ ins
(26 x 19.8 cm)
Bequest of Henry Walters, 1931; Inc. B-142 (B-127), folio 105v

The rare earliest Dutch edition of the *De proprietatibus
rerum*, a fourteenth-century encyclopedia, was published
by Haarlem's first printer, Jakob Bellaert (active late
fifteenth century). Each section of the book in The
Walters' copy is illustrated with a full-page, carefully
hand-colored woodcut. This cut illustrates the discourse
on the ages of man. Infancy, childhood, adolescence,
youth, maturity, old age, and death are all personified in
the upper portion of the image. Below, a physician
examines a urine sample at a sick person's bedside and a
surgeon operates on a hapless patient.

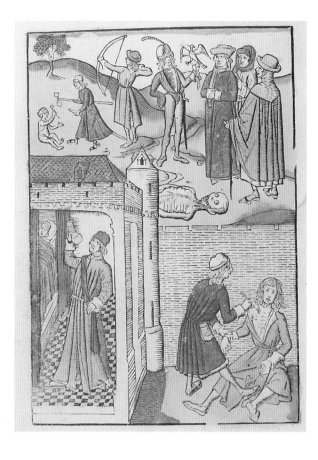

Pietro Andrea Mattioli, **Commentarii in Dioscoridis De**
Materia Medica (Commentary on Dioscorides, On
Medical Matters, Volume I): Orange
(Italian, Venice, Vincenzo Valgrisi, 1565)
Ink on paper with watercolor washes, 13 ⅜ x 9 ¼ ins
(34 x 21.2 cm)
Museum Purchase, 1991; B-7, page 245

As they gained a renewed interest in botany,
Renaissance scholars turned their attention to the work
of Dioscorides, the ancient Greek authority. They also
described plants unknown in antiquity: the orange tree,
for example, had originated in China. Mattioli's
Commentary on Dioscorides, first published by Vincenzo
Valgrisi in 1544, was one of the most popular herbals
of the sixteenth century. This edition was the first to
contain the full series of over 900 large, detailed, elegant
woodcuts produced by Giorgio Liberale (active 1560s)
and Wolfgang Meyerpeck.

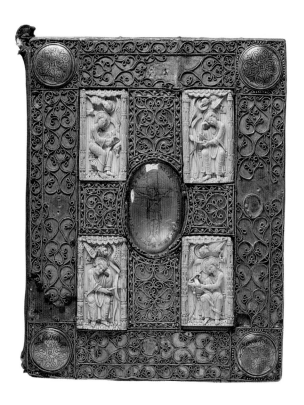

Gospel Lectionary (The Mondsee Gospels): Treasure Binding

(German, Regensburg, third quarter of the eleventh century)
Ivory, rock crystal, silver filigree, silver gilt filigree and niello,
11 x 18 ½ ins (27.9 x 21.8 cm)
Bequest of Henry Walters, 1931; MS W.8, front cover

The heavy oak boards of this precious book cover are decorated with silver filigree plaques, of which the four central ones are gilded, forming a cross. Gems have been lost from the border. In the corners are silver bosses with a design in niello. Four carved ivory plaques represent the Evangelists writing or reading in their studies, while their respective winged symbols descend from above (St. Luke, at the lower left, is a modern replacement modeled on St. John at the upper right). At the center a cabochon crystal covers a painting of the Crucifixion on gold leaf, an unusual medieval attempt to imitate the ancient technique of working gold leaf under glass. Exceptionally, the original structure and sewing of the binding are still intact. The spine is covered with contemporary silk damask of Byzantine or Middle Eastern origin.

Lacquered Binding with Hunting Scenes: *Jami*, **Divan** (Poems)

(Iran, early seventeenth century)
Watercolor and varnish on pasteboard,
10 ½ x 11 ⁵⁄₁₆ ins (27 x 29.5 cm)
Bequest of Henry Walters, 1931;
MS W.640, back cover and flap

The creation of leather bindings, generally ornamented with stamped and gilded designs, had developed as an integral part of the Islamic arts of the book by at least the ninth century, if not earlier. Beginning in the late fifteenth century, the decoration of bookbindings in Iran expanded to include compositions painted in watercolor and varnished with layers of clear lacquer. This fine example, enclosing poems by Abdul-Rahman Jami (1414–92), depicts hunters on foot and horseback pursuing prey of various species. The protective triangular flap represents a hunter preparing to skin a gazelle buck.

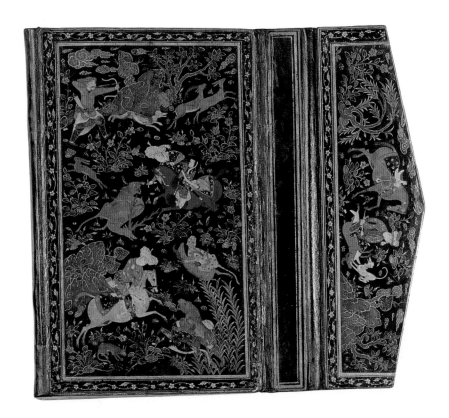